KU-444-187

AMAZON TASK FORCE

AMAZON TASK FORCE

PETER DIXON

in collaboration with

DICK BELL

HODDER AND STOUGHTON
LONDON SYDNEY AUCKLAND TORONTO

British Library Cataloguing in Publication Data
Dixon, Peter
    Amazon task force.
    1. Joint Services Hovercraft Expedition to
       Peru, *1982*   2. Amazon River   3. Peru—
       Description and travel—1981–
    I. Title
    918.5'4304633'0924   F3425

ISBN 0 340 32713 8 (cased); 0 340 34578 0 (paper)

Copyright © 1984 by Peter Dixon. First printed 1984. All rights reserved. No part of this publication may be reproduced or transmitted in any form or by any means, electronic or mechanical, including photocopy, recording, or any information storage and retrieval system, without permission in writing from the publisher. Printed in Great Britain for Hodder and Stoughton Limited, Mill Road, Dunton Green, Sevenoaks, Kent by St. Edmundsbury Press, Bury St. Edmunds, Suffolk. Typeset by Hewer Text Composition Services, Edinburgh.

Hodder and Stoughton Editorial Office: 47 Bedford Square, London WC1B 3DP.

Contents

Illustrations

Photography by Stu Antrobus and other team members.

Foreword

By the Rt. Hon. Edward Heath, M.B.E., M.P.

This is a splendid story of a Mission thoroughly well organised and brilliantly executed, whose immediate purpose was fully accomplished. It makes exciting reading.

The expedition was not just an intrepid venture against considerable odds over the rivers of Peru. It also set out to bring help and succour to some of the poorest people in the world, uncared for, grievously afflicted by sickness, and un-versed in even the simplest aspects of agricultural production.

To those sceptical of official reports on the situation in the developing world, these pages describe the often appalling conditions encountered by the team. The urgent need was for such basic elements as clean water and preventative medicine. For those who ask what can be done to help and how these problems should be handled this book provides some of the clues.

The President of Peru expressed his deep gratitude to the British team for the assistance they had provided for his country and for the example they had set. We should thank the author and his colleagues for bringing the story home so vividly to us and for showing us so plainly how much still remains to be done.

Acknowledgments

Although it is my name that appears on the cover, in fact this book belongs to the team. That would be true in any event, since it is the exploits of a band of men and women that are described here. However, in this case it is doubly so. In putting the story together, I used the reminiscences, written or spoken, of almost every member of the team. However, one member's contribution was even greater. Dick Bell scrupulously kept a detailed diary in Peru, and later spent countless hours working on his narrative, at the expense of his busy conference centre and printing business. Without his selfless work this book would have been nothing.

Naturally, I am also eternally indebted to the other team members. Without too much searching, they will find much of themselves in this book. In the preparation of the manuscript, I was relieved to have two superb typists – Anne Penman, who busied herself in farthest Wales producing coherent initial drafts from the scribblings I sent her, and Joan Edlin, who worked in her home near Mansfield to prepare the immaculate final draft. No less helpful (and patient) were the staff of Hodder and Stoughton, especially Louise Tulip, Carolyn Armitage and Rob Warner. Back home, my wife Ingrid was as patient as Job while the house filled up with mountains of paper, much of which she had to proof-read.

Finally, though, I thank Mike Cole: for his contribution to this book; for his drive, determination and faith, which made the expedition and the book possible, and for the privilege of working with him for the past five years.

Cranwell, April 1983   Peter Dixon

CHAPTER ONE

Jungle Fever

PAUL WATSON WAS in pain. He had been feeling the pains in his stomach for nearly a week. By Sunday afternoon they were excruciating. Even when well he could not be described as plump. But now his thin face was gaunt and drawn. Through the night he had slept only fitfully, and on Monday morning he was too weary and disturbed by pain to make his way to the workshop. The other engineers had to work without his help.

By Tuesday morning Dr. Bill Gould, who had been watching Paul for twenty-four hours, had diagnosed one of two alternatives: either it was appendicitis or it was a typhoid condition with ulceration. Restriction to fluids and treatment with antibiotics had done little to improve the situation, and now this young man was seriously ill. Paul would have to go into the local hospital for an operation.

But matters were not that simple. The local hospital had an operating room that had indeed once seen operations, but now the austere concrete walls housed only the most rudimentary facilities. There was no proper anaesthetic. No facilities existed for sterilising the equipment, and, in any case, if there were to be an operation, Bill would have to do it himself. For this was not England, where a simple 999 call would bring an ambulance racing along the road. Paul Watson had been taken ill in the remote jungle of Peru. He was a member of a Joint Services Expedition, and he had forsaken, for a season, the comfortable trappings of civilisation.

The nearest suitable hospital was in Ayacucho, ten hours away on one of the bumpiest roads in the world. A harrowing,

COLOMBIA

ECUADOR

Caracas

● Bogotá

PERU

Lima

SOUTH
AMERICA

●D

R.Amazon

R.Marañon

BRAZIL

R.Ucayali

Pucallpa ●

Atalaya ●

R.Urubamba

San Francisco ●

LIMA ●

● Machu Picchu

Ayacucho ● ● Cuzco

● Pisco

● Nazca

L.Titicaca

● Arequipa

PACIFIC
OCEAN

BOLIVIA

CHILE

perhaps even fatal, experience for a critically ill patient. Even this hospital, though, had only limited facilities.

The only answer was to fly the patient out to the sophisticated hospitals in the capital, Lima. That at least was practical; the suffering Paul was lying in his tent only yards from a rough rutted airstrip. But there was no telephone. We had to walk to the jungle town's bank and send a message by radio asking for an aircraft to be sent.

Once the plane was under way, the Lima Bank telephoned the British Embassy asking them to arrange an ambulance to meet it. The Defence Attaché rushed with an ambulance to Lima airport, but when the plane landed neither patient nor doctor was aboard.

The Peruvian pilot explained that he had not been able to land at our jungle base, which was covered by low cloud and heavy rain. We had only a simple unlighted airstrip, and, of course, there was no Instrument Landing System or radar. And the mountains around us were very high; some of the clouds could have very hard centres! Paul had to spend yet another feverish night in his uncomfortable camp bed.

By now Paul was very weak; he was receiving fluids intravenously, and it was clear to the doctor that the appendix or an ulcer had burst, allowing fluid into his peritoneal cavity. He was suffering the intense pain of peritonitis.

Wednesday morning once more brought dull overcast skies. The Embassy had asked the Peruvian Air Force for help, and we spent the morning waiting expectantly to hear the characteristic slap-slap of a helicopter. It never came. Later we heard that attempts had been made, but the Air Force had been unable to get through the cloud-covered mountain passes.

The night passed quietly, with members of the team praying earnestly for a solution. Meanwhile, the Embassy staff in Lima feared that Thursday's story would be no better. For three days foul storms had raged through the Andes. In any case, Thursday was National Civil Aviation Day; most of the pilots planned to be at a fiesta.

It was with scepticism that the authorities in Lima received our weather report on Thursday morning. 'We are looking up at high, well-broken cloud,' I transmitted in frustration. 'Half

13

of the sky is blue. Where is that plane?' In Lima they thought we must be dreaming; a line of thunderstorm activity virtually covered the whole of the Peruvian Andes. The Embassy gave us more credence. If the line of storms could be crossed, they thought, then the clearing weather over the jungle opened up the possibility of success. They searched out a charter company with sober pilots and persuaded them to give it a try. Encouraged by reports confirming our view of the weather, they were spurred on by a further message from us: Paul's fever was once again worsening.

Bill Gould started to talk about scrubbing down the camp mess table for surgery. Knowing that a pilot would want daylight to attempt to cross the mountains, we were resigned by mid-afternoon to the idea of the risky operation.

At exactly five p.m., someone in the camp shouted 'Quiet! I can hear a plane!' One by one, the others agreed. Then we could see it. After a few low passes to check the airstrip for animals, the white Cessna 402 touched down on the grass, bringing three days of tension to an end.

The plane was immediately surrounded by a horde of inquisitive children, fingering the bright paintwork. A twin-engined plane was a rare sight here. The swarthy ex-Air Force pilot was worried about the length of the airstrip, some 1,200 metres, and sent his co-pilot to pace out the distance. Meanwhile, Paul was carried from his tent on a stretcher, grinning weakly as Bill Gould held an intravenous drip over him. While they settled down in the aircraft, the team cleared the sheep and cattle which had ambled back on to the airstrip. We cleared the craning bystanders away from the propellers, but as soon as the plane had turned and lined up for take-off, the children gleefully ran behind it to feel the slipstream pressing against their bodies. The pilot looked round anxiously, but shrugged as he realised he could do nothing about the reckless *chicitos*. He increased to full power, rolled along the bumpy strip, and within a minute Paul was on his way to Lima and health. We heard the next day that the plane had arrived at six fifty p.m.; at ten p.m. Paul had been operated upon for 'peritonitis with tropical complications', with complete success. The initial cause had been appendicitis; the appendix

14

removed by the expatriate German surgeon was already gangrenous.

Weeks passed before Corporal Paul Watson was in a fit condition to fly home to England. Today he is fully recovered, but he played no further part in our work.

As the plane climbed out of the valley and receded into the evening sky, I reflected on Paul's departure with mixed feelings. Relief, of course; the uneasy realisation, too, of how far we were from help if things went wrong; but also a sense of privilege in the level of sophisticated medicine we were used to. Those who called the Amazon home could expect no such treatment.

My own involvement had begun some four years before, in 1978. On the other side of the world, in the mysterious Himalayan kingdom of Nepal, was another river. The Kali Gandaki, the 'Goddess of death', was swift, treacherous and unnavigable for much of its length; and Mike Cole, a Physical Education officer in the R.A.F., had a burning ambition to turn it into a highway. But not just for the sake of adventure: he wanted to prove that the people of the river were not too remote to get medical help. Mike felt that the only craft which could successfully overcome the rapids and the shallows was a hovercraft – a very special hovercraft called the River Rover.

River Rover had been made for the job. Although it had started its life in a garage in Gosport, it was designed by missionary engineer Tim Longley as the Land Rover of the river, with seating for six and powered by an efficient and reliable 2165 cc Renault car engine. A hovercraft can skim over water and land where boats cannot go, but its cushion of air makes it a difficult creature to control. Not River Rover. With the sharp bends and tortuous channels of a Himalayan river in mind, this craft had been given a unique control system with which the machine could be turned tightly and manoeuvred positively in the turbulent white water.

Two of these craft formed the core of the Joint Services Hovercraft Expedition to Nepal in 1978–9. My place in the team was as the junior hovercraft pilot – a far cry from my normal work, at that time, flying Hercules transports. Under

15

Mike Cole's enthusiastic, ebullient leadership, we proved that the hovercraft really could navigate the violent Kali Gandaki.[1] But Mike's vision – to set up a long term 'hovering doctor' service, bringing medical care to the unreachable – had not been fulfilled. The little mission hospital in the Himalayan foothills, whose director, Dr. Bill Gould, had first suggested that hovercraft might navigate the river, lacked the facilities to make use of the River Rover long-term. Once the expedition was over, we brought the craft out of Nepal.

For nearly two years, the feeling that the project was incomplete was with us. Then Mike received a message from the Overseas Development Administration, part of the Foreign Office. Could we set up a 'hovering doctor' service in the Peruvian jungle?

Peru. I would not exactly say that I had to look it up in the atlas, but my knowledge of it was certainly sketchy. I knew the name of the capital, and of course I knew where Paddington Bear had come from. Beyond that, I was in the dark.

I set about planning a reconnaissance visit for Mike and myself. The date chose itself. Mike's current Initial Officer Training Course finished in mid-June, and I had to be with my Squadron on their summer detachment on the last day of June. The gap of two weeks gave us very little time. I put together an itinerary and searched around for the cheapest way to get to Lima. The accepted wisdom was to cross the Atlantic to Miami and change flights there. This I booked, but by the time I realised that the travel agent had reserved seats for the wrong date, the date we wanted was fully booked. What to do? Meanwhile, British Caledonian, smarting from the loss of business, had dropped their London–Lima fare to £1 less than the combined fare I was paying. Less to pay, and a direct flight too. As it turned out, the apparent coincidence did not just save us money and time; it was the start of a relationship with British Caledonian Airways which did much for the success of the project.

It was not until we were actually on our way to Gatwick Airport that Mike added another complication to what had

[1] This story has been told by the B.B.C. in their film *Journey to the Fourth World*, and in Michael Cole's book of the same name.

seemed the perfectly straightforward procedure of getting on to an aeroplane.

'I have been asked to take a spare part to the people we are meeting,' explained my tall, energetic companion. 'It's for a jet boat which is working on the river in the jungle area.' Fine, I thought, but I wasn't prepared for the giant carton, which towered over Mike as he brought it on an airport trolley from Gatwick station. The check-in staff were taken aback too, and I recalled the essential asset needed when travelling with Mike Cole: a flexible mind.

Lima's population figure of 4¾ million inhabitants is little more than an educated guess. With every succeeding day the city's boundaries creep a little further out into the desert. Nobody really knows how many live in the vast, sprawling *pueblos jóvenes*, the euphemistically named 'young villages'. We would call them slums. The casual visitor to Lima knows nothing of this. Scornfully turning away the hawker or the shoe-shine boy, how is he to know what conditions they will go home to? The elegant shopping arcades and multi-storey hotels lay a veneer of prosperity over the metropolis.

We were met at Lima's Jorge Chaves airport by Julian Latham, the man whose selfless work was the reason for our coming to Peru. The broad-shouldered Rhodesian shook us firmly by the hand and introduced us to a representative from the British Embassy, who had taken the trouble to come out to meet us on this Saturday night.

While Mike and Julian discussed plans for the next few days, I waited to check out the luggage as it came through from the aircraft. There was little chance of confusion as ours was the only flight using the sleepy airport at that time of night. But when the flow of suitcases and rucksacks had dried up I was still standing there, waiting for one more item – the 90-kilogram parcel. A pretty young ground hostess, whose Latin features seemed incongruous with the tartan airline uniform, found the answer. Our over-sized piece of luggage still had the British Rail Red Star labels on it, consigning it to London Gatwick Airport. Naturally enough, the Peruvian airport workers had left it on the plane to go back there. And that wasn't the last trouble it caused. Julian later spent a whole week trying to get the letter from Ministry of Health to the Customs authorities, so that he could have it released from the airport. That was a mild foretaste of what someone once said is Peru's national sport – bureaucracy.

During our drive to the hotel Julian filled us in on Peruvian driving technique. For instance, all traffic lights are considered to be advisory rather than compulsory. Priority at a junction seems to go to the driver who has most nerve. There are traffic policemen, but they seem to fight a losing battle, and in any case are held in very little respect. Julian told us a story to illustrate the techniques the police adopted. He had a vehicle which was registered in Lima, but kept in the Apurímac valley on the other side of the Andes, and it had never actually been in Lima. Nevertheless, he managed to get a parking ticket for it for parking illegally in Lima. His number had been picked at random, but he still found that the onus was on him to prove his innocence.

By the time we arrived at the hotel we had been on the move for over twenty-four hours and it was three thirty a.m. 'body-time'. But even then we were not able to sink gratefully into bed. The hotel receptionist knew nothing of our reservation and claimed that the hotel was completely full. Finally, room was found. By then, it did not matter that it was a single room with a camp bed added. Mike, as the Squadron Leader, got the bed. I, the Flight Lieutenant, volunteered for the camp bed.

In preparation for our coming trip to the jungle, we bought maps of the area from the *Instituto Geográfico Militar*, and visited Captain Malcolm Carver, R.N., then the Defence Attaché at the Lima Embassy, finding a true gentleman who brought to our project his enthusiastic support.

Before we left for the jungle, I took the opportunity to confirm our flight home and found that we were fortunate to have seats booked. Anyone who could think of an excuse for leaving Lima that week was doing so because a well known American seismologist had predicted an earthquake which would be centred just off the coast; it would be as heavy as any earthquake that Peru had seen in its history. Giant tidal waves would sweep away the city on the day after we were due to fly out. Needless to say, it didn't in fact happen, but the prediction was taken seriously in the city, and the atmosphere was tense and uncertain.

On Wednesday we were up early to catch the flight to Ayacucho in the heart of the Andes mountains, with Julian as our guide. We had booked seats on the AeroPeru flight for seven o'clock that morning but, of course, we had not known the Peruvian way of doing things. In fact, there were two flights. The earlier one, not published to the world, left at six forty-five a.m. If there were not enough custom, the second, the internationally published one, would be cancelled. We had in Julian an excellent local adviser, and were there in good time for the first flight.

Only forty minutes of flying took us across the bulk of the Andes range to the 9,000-feet-high airport of Ayacucho. The old colonial city, with its cathedral and its central square, has two main claims to fame: its history and its terrorists. The battle of Ayacucho in 1824, in fact fought at nearby Quinua, was decisive in the expulsion from Peru of the Spanish *Conquistadores* by Bolívar; and the strength of terrorism in the region would cause us plenty of problems in the coming year. The name of the town means 'Dead Man's Corner'.

The distance from Ayacucho to San Francisco on the Apurímac river is only about fifty miles as the condor flies, but by road the distance is 150 miles, taking a gruelling eight hours by Land Rover. The Andes contain some of the most difficult stretches of road in the world. For most of its length, this road has a dirt surface and snakes its way across the mountainside, reaching 15,000 feet as it crosses the Sacsahuilca range of mountains. Here herds of llama graze peacefully on the sparse covering of grass, tended by hardy Quechua Indians in brightly coloured poncho blankets and sombre hats. At these altitudes cacti of every type abound. The high plateau, or *altiplano*, is too bleak and windswept to support real agriculture, or even cattle. The only animals which can be grazed are llamas, alpacas and, sometimes, sheep. The wool from here, and the brightly coloured garments which the Indians weave from it, provide a little extra income, but the hardy Indians mostly have to support themselves directly from their flocks.

As the road starts to descend from the heights, on the far side of the 15,000-foot pass, the scrub supported by the thin topsoil gradually gives way to dense jungle. Trees, like the road, cling tenuously to near-vertical slopes. The secondary jungle is rich and thick around the road, and when it rains the road turns into a lethal mud bath. Then the underlying fertility of what appears to be no more than dust becomes apparent.

As Julian drove us carefully and slowly along the bumpy road, he pointed out the places where close friends had been killed as trucks or cars fell hundreds of feet from the dirt track. Simple crosses marked these spots, and those of other accidents, and in places the wreckage was still visible as a splash of colour in the monotony of jungle-green. For the people of the jungle, death is ever present. There are few who have not lost a father or son, a brother or a sister.

But road travel is not the only killer in the *selva*, the jungle to the east of the Andes. Snakes and tarantulas claim their victims. Disease of every kind is rife. And then there is the river itself. The Rio Apurímac flows fast and furious from the mountains which were once the home of the Inca civilisation. It winds northwards through the hills, passing under its final bridge at San Francisco, until it joins the Rio Tambo and the Rio Ene, to become just one of the hundreds of rivers which drain half of South America into the Amazon.

By then, of course, the river is wide and calm, but the quantity of water is enormous. At Iquitos, in Northern Peru, the river is two or three miles wide, yet the river level can vary as much as thirty feet. Back at San Francisco the change is smaller, but still enough to wash away houses close to the river when the rains come between October and March.

Even further upstream the river is a complex system of shallows, whirlpools and awesome rapids. It constantly changes as the water level varies. The boatmen who steer their craft through the white water make their skilled art look deceptively simple. Nevertheless, dozens of lives are lost each year to the river's fury.

This valley was our destination.

For Peru, the jungle is a modern-day Wild West. The fertile

river valleys are a magnet to the Quechua Indians, eking out their livelihood from the bare earth of the *altiplano*. They hack out a tract of ground from the dense jungle and bring their families to settle on their new homestead. They combine into communities and villages, becoming towns such as San Francisco, a market town which is essential to the valley's young economy. Once they have somewhere to live and something to eat, the settlers start to think of other essential needs. The most important is health. After years of selfless work for the people of the Apurímac valley, Julian became a catalyst in providing rudimentary health care.

The first part of his project involved converting an empty shell of a building into a working hospital. When we visited the *Centro de Salud de San Francisco* it was in full swing. Simple consulting rooms and maternity ward; a dental surgery (for extractions only – there was no equipment for fillings or crowns); a small pharmacy with half-empty shelves; and tiny wards with patients ranging from cases of tuberculosis to a baby girl with a horrific tarantula bite.

Most known diseases are endemic in the river area, and several unknown ones too. Even to wade in the river brings danger from the parasites it harbours. Accidental injuries bring tetanus, and the vampire bats which move soundlessly through the night air almost always transmit rabies when they bite humans. Many patients arrive at San Francisco too late to be treated effectively, because there are few roads.

Once the hospital was under way with Peruvian staff, the way was open to take simple health care out to the villages. Handing over the hospital to the Ministry of Health would release the resources needed. Julian raised the cash for building materials for health posts in the major villages. Each community erected its own building, and chose a young villager to go to San Francisco for nine months of training. When we arrived in the valley, some of these *sanitarios* were ready to return and care for the health of their communities.

Over the next four days we visited villages up and down the river, listening to speeches of welcome, speeches of thanks, speeches of petition. We received simple village hospitality as the three-way interpretations made their slow progress: a fried egg on a bed of rice and onions; fresh orange juice – scooped from a white enamel bucket – in a glass which was shared by all present. We, the honoured visitors, received the cup first – fine until the cup came round for the second time!

Visiting one village, Villa Virgen, we brought with us the newly-qualified *sanitaria*, Rebecca. The villagers lined up proudly to receive a painful injection from the girl they had chosen, as she stood there in her clean white uniform.

That night we slept on a concrete floor in the village of Lechemayo; cockroaches fell dead to the floor around us through the night, knocked out by insecticide spray. Before four a.m. we were awakened by a battle between the cockerels on our side of the square and an ear-splitting radio on the other. The cockerels won. At five a.m. they were joined by a lone chanting voice. Eventually I made out the words: '*Carretera Lechemayo! Carretera Lechemayo!*' It was what in Grosvenor Square would have been called a demo, asking these powerful foreigners to get a road built to Lechemayo. But who could blame the man, however drunk he was? When the village had been hit by disease some years earlier, forty-nine people had died – probably from typhoid or yellow fever – before help could arrive from San Francisco.

'The road could take years to reach Lechemayo,' groaned Julian. It was becoming obvious that River Rover was badly needed. If we could set up a permanent 'hovering doctor' service here, the project's loose end, left hanging on the other side of the world, would be tied. Our plans for another 'expedition with a purpose' were crystallising here on the Amazon.

In each village the beaming pride on the faces of the Quechua farmers, as they showed us their bright new buildings, was a tribute both to their own determination to help themselves and to Julian Latham's years of thankless, unrelenting effort. Even more encouraging was the health post at Otari, built jointly by Quechua settlers and primitive jungle Indians of the Campa tribe. Among the simple thatched shelters in which they lived stood the neat concrete building. Like other communities, these primitive hunters would have a health worker drawn from their own people.

From the Campas, too, there was hospitality. Their chief offered a gourd filled with *masatu*, which was fine until we learned how it was made. The women of the tribe sit around a giant bowl chewing manioc and spitting the masticated pulp into the bowl. After a few days the fermented liquid is ready for drinking. Squadron Leader Michael Cole returned to Britain to plan the Joint Services Hovercraft Expedition to Peru, with the taste of the Amazon in his mouth.

CHAPTER TWO

Before the Storm

THE SUCCESS OR failure of an expedition can often be determined long before departure. Almost the first step is to put together the right team; it is the step on which success depends. For a 'simple' task like climbing Everest, for instance, whole philosophies have built up around team composition. Climbers divide into two opposing camps.

The old way involved a large team, laying siege to the mountain with scores of support climbers, so as to put a pair on to the summit. But the weight of numbers brings its own problems, as the team becomes bogged down in its own sluggishness. The purists of the mountaineering world, therefore, put together small close-knit teams of expert climbers, unhampered by the problems of administration and major finance, and able to concentrate on the primary goal. This concept's development culminated in Reinhold Messner's solo Everest climb in 1980.

Mike Cole could not afford such a luxury. As I sat with him on the British Caledonian DC 10, flying back to London, we agreed that our task had too many facets for a small team to succeed.

'Good administration is the key,' he said 'especially during the preparation phase. The team will have to be organised on military lines, with separate sections for the different tasks. I know just the man to be chief administrator.'

Although I had not then met Chris Bunney, I later learned how right Mike was. Tall, lean and bespectacled, Chris was blessed with a no-nonsense sense of humour which could

24

at times develop into biting sarcasm. He had worked for Mike at Cranwell and impressed him with his brisk, efficient organisation. Recently promoted to Squadron Leader, he was working at the R.A.F.'s computerised personnel centre in Gloucester. Mike later offered him a place on the expedition, and although Chris sometimes disagreed with Mike's Christian grounds for his actions, that never prevented him from lending his full support to the leader.

'That builds us up to three,' I said. 'What about those who were with us in Nepal?' The team that had tested the hovercraft on the Kali Gandaki river had been brimming with talent. 'We need some of that River Rover experience.'

'Yes,' said my companion, 'but we must leave room for new blood.'

We chatted about those who had kept up their interest in the project since our return in the spring of 1979. There was Tony Maher, the Royal Marine sergeant who had proved himself as much at home running an office in London as he was in a turbulent Himalayan rapid, although he made no secret of which he preferred. Fiercely proud of his Royal Marine background, he longed to taste every experience and fight in every battle. He was a professional, and fully deserved the place that Mike later offered him.

At the other end of the seagoing spectrum, approaching retirement after a long career of Royal Naval service, was white-bearded Lieutenant Commander Brian Holdsworth. Mike had chosen him to act as the U.K. link man for the early part of the Nepal expedition; his meticulous eye for fine detail and his methodical approach to problems had ensured that every spare part or document we needed had appeared in Nepal as quickly as was humanly possible. Brian was a perfectionist; if something did not seem quite right to him, he would not be satisfied until a tidy solution was reached.

'If Brian would agree to lead the rear party again,' mused Mike, 'we couldn't do better.' A few weeks later, the offer was made and enthusiastically accepted.

The leader of a Service expedition has considerable freedom to choose his team. Although he is expected by the Joint

Services Expedition Trust to avail as many as possible of the opportunity to participate, he cannot be censured for choosing some team members whose qualities he knows at first hand. Set up in 1960 to encourage adventurous projects, on the far-sighted premise that adventure makes good training, the Trust casts a critical eye over all proposed major expeditions in the Services. Our plans would have to be scrutinised before we could go ahead.

After our homecoming, Mike returned to his office work in the Ministry of Defence, using his spare time to prepare a detailed proposal for the Peruvian expedition, while I returned to my Squadron.

The plans took shape in the autumn of 1981. The primary aim of the team, of course, would be to link up the village clinics by hovercraft. But it was not enough simply to serve the clinics for a few months and then leave, allowing them to return to their former isolation. The service had to have a lasting effect, and to that end we would need to train Peruvians to drive and maintain the craft.

'We will have a four-pronged organisation, Peter,' said Mike as we sat at his desk one Monday, drinking coffee from cracked cups. 'I want you to look after all of the operation of hovercraft and boats on the river, and organise the pilot training. There will be an engineering team, a strong medical team, and Chris Bunney's administrators.'

The project was expanding beyond my expectations, if not Mike's, but it seemed right that it should. Before leaving Peru, we had talked with Julian about the needs of the valley, which extended beyond the mere provision of a river transport system. Mike had caught the persistent Rhodesian's vision. For years Julian had laboured to bring health and life and dignity to the valley people. His work had been partly supported by British Government aid, through the charitable Amazon Trust, and the British connection had brought much goodwill for Britain in the region. We would be bringing considerable human resources to the Apurímac, and the opportunity was there for us to attack the people's problems on a broad front. Properly directed, our short-term assistance could be a powerful shot in the arm for Julian's permanent work, and its effects would continue to be felt long after we had departed. Mike was determined to think big.

To do justice to the Apurímac medical services, he had decided to supply two of the new Mark 3 River Rovers instead of one. In order to keep our lines of communication open along the dirt road from Ayacucho, we would need a rugged four-wheel drive vehicle for the period of the expedition. Mike arranged to take out a V8 Land Rover which we could hand over to Julian at the end of our time in the valley.

The hovercraft and other equipment would need to be housed. Julian had at first planned a 'hover-garage' and had undertaken to have it built before our arrival if we could raise the cash for it. Later, after Mike had spoken with Colin Roth of the O.D.A., the Overseas Development Administration of the Foreign Office, and obtained financial agreement, the plans for the building expanded until it was a full-scale operations centre, including medical stores and accommodation for medical staff.

To link up the health posts with each other and with the hovercraft by radio, we would need to buy fourteen high-frequency transceivers, battery operated, and the aerial arrays to go with them. Even the lowest quotation came to £14,000. These and many other expenses were necessary if we were to achieve that lasting benefit which was our ambition.

In September 1981 the planned expedition budget stood at £120,000. Expeditions are not normally supported from public funds, so although some of the expenditure had been promised by O.D.A., the rest had to be raised from commercial sources. Each member of the team would have to make a substantial contribution to the funds, so we were not asking anyone to subsidise a free holiday for us. Even so, we seemed to have picked the worst possible time for our mission of innovation and adventure. Would it be possible to raise the sort of money we were thinking of, in a time of defence cuts and recession? The prospect was daunting, and weighed heavily on Mike Cole's shoulders, but it was not long before he received a dramatic encouragement.

Towards the end of the Nepal expedition, Mike and I had met a successful and dynamic businessman named Colin Reilly,

27

in Kathmandu. In the autumn of 1981, Mike visited him in his Lake District home and described our plans for Peru. Nailing his colours firmly to the mast, Colin dared to mention 'hover-craft' under 'Any Other Business' at a busy board meeting of N.S.S., a national chain of newsagents.

The chemistry of raising support is not open to clinical analysis. It was necessary to gain at least a sympathetic hearing for our 'unusual adventure' in a forum where sound business decisions are the order of the day. To gain a few fleeting well-rehearsed moments with the executive at the top is essential. Colin Reilly's courage had made this possible.

In the heart of the business area of the City of London, Mike was shown into a panelled reception room, the decor radiating commercial confidence. He dusted his unusually highly polished shoes, expecting a frosty hearing at best.

'I did enjoy your book,' said the secretary to a bemused Mike as she showed him into her boss's office.

Mr. Philip Byam-Cook, a generous City mandarin and chairman both of a charitable trust and of N.S.S. Newsagents, greeted Mike warmly.

'Now,' he said, 'just how are we going to help you?'

His City trust made a generous grant and N.S.S. arranged to publish a special colour edition of *Journey to the Fourth World*, with the proceeds going to the expedition budget.

One aspect of our plans for Peru, which had not even entered our heads when we started our visit, turned out to be the most exciting. As we passed through Lima on the way home, we had shared our hopes and plans for the Apurímac with Dr. Stewart Mackintosh, a Scottish missionary with R.B.M.U., the Regions Beyond Missionary Union. Stewart had spent many years working in Peru, and now taught at the Evangelical Seminary in Lima. With his enthusiastic interest in the right sort of technology, and his encyclopaedic knowledge of South America, he quickly warmed to the idea of using hovercraft on Peru's rivers.

'This could be just the right thing for the Peruvian Church,' he explained. 'They would love to extend their work into the jungle, and support the local churches in the Amazon basin and the mountains. The communities are isolated. They need

28

to be linked up with each other, and your hovercraft could be the answer.'

We besieged Stewart with questions.

'Where could the River Rover be based?'

'Probably at Pucallpa. It could serve a very wide area from there.'

'Who would operate the machine?'

'There's an organisation called C.E.M.A.A. (Evangelical Centre for Andean and Amazonian Missiology) which helps the Peruvian church groups to do work that has traditionally been done by missionaries. They could probably co-ordinate the effort.'

'Who would pay for it?'

'Ah.' Stewart paused. 'There you have me.'

'No problem,' smiled Mike. 'I have always found that if something is the right thing to do, the money for it is forth-coming.'

The planning went no further while we were in Lima, but the more Mike and I thought about the idea, the more enthusi-astic we became. This could be the ideal finale to the expedition, for to move the hovercraft from San Francisco to Pucallpa involved a 1,000-kilometre journey into the heart of Amazonia. Although our plans for the Apurímac included an attempt to push up the treacherous river just as far as the River Rover could take us, we had to admit that the project as planned so far was heavy on hard work and light on adventure! The journey to Pucallpa, the longest ever completed by a light hovercraft, would redress the balance.

The Amazon journey fitted perfectly into Mike's personal tradition of adventurous Christian endeavour. But his financial confidence had yet to be proved. He himself had no doubts that God would provide the finance: it had happened so many times before. Even before Peru had entered the picture, for instance, he had received a research award from the Leverhulme Trust to enable his concept of Third World communications to be developed further. Even so, I had less faith and looked forward to seeing the financial needs securely met.

Our first encouragement came quickly. The modest profits of the package holiday organisers, Highway Travel, go to the charitable Highway Trust, and in 1980 a very successful Oberammergau season had produced an unusually sizeable income for the Trust. The Chairman, Chris Scott, a retired Lieutenant Colonel of the Royal Army Service Corps, and the Trustees pledged themselves to finance one River Rover hovercraft for the pioneering journey through Amazonia.

We saw our budget further expanded as diverse gifts in kind, such as engines and spares, oil, jungle footwear, medicines, free use of a shipping container, and the printing of 4,000 attractive first day covers, were added to the essential financial grant from O.D.A. The project was also backed by hundreds of individual supporters which ensured the provision of £150,000.

Sometimes persistence paid off. 'Yes, you'll get your equipment,' barked one busy executive to Tony Maher, 'just stop phoning me!'

The encouragements were timely, for there were battles ahead. Although our innovative hovercraft were creating jobs on the Isle of Wight where they were built, and River Rovers had been ordered by an overseas police force and the Australian Army, there was no direct defence benefit to the Royal Air Force.

'Royal Navy in Distress' read the Autumn 1981 headlines, referring to the proposed defence cuts. A parliamentary question was put down by an M.P. from a dockyard constituency. Why had Colonel John Blashford-Snell, leader of the successful venture 'Operation Drake', been allowed to participate in such an expedition at this time of financial stringency? The remarkable Colonel, enjoying Royal patronage, was well able to parry such a thrust, but the question sparked an investigation of the R.A.F. by senior civil servants. The hovercraft expedition came under close critical scrutiny, but finally the project sailed through stormy waters into the spring of 1982.

Preparations were gathering pace. Mike had circulated details throughout the Services and applications were flooding on to his desk for the three-month expedition, which was due to start on May 1st, 1982. Among them came a signal from the Defence Attaché in Lima:

'WILL BE FULLY OCCUPIED WITH PROPOSED

ROYAL VISIT MAY 82. SUPPORT FOR YOU WILL BE
LIMITED. REGRET THIS BRICKBAT.'

An idea for an answer to the bureaucracy which was squeez-
ing the project took Mike's imagination by storm.

'THIS IS A BOUQUET, NOT A BRICKBAT,' he signalled back. 'PLEASE ASK HRH PRINCESS ALEXANDRA
IF SHE WOULD CONSIDER REVIEWING OUR
HOVERCRAFT ON DISPLAY IN LIMA.' His suggestion
was readily accepted.

We now planned to take four River Rovers to Peru. There
were three new Mark 3 craft, two for San Francisco and one
for Pucallpa. But in addition we would take to the Apurímac a
Mark 2 craft which had been with us in Nepal; it had been
lovingly refurbished as a spare-time project by the apprentices
of the Civilian Engineering School at R.A.F. St. Athan.

Our Land Rover-sized hovercraft would fit perfectly into
the freight hold of an R.A.F. Hercules aircraft, and Mike asked
that a crew-training flight might be diverted to meet our needs.
However, a training flight to Peru was a non-starter in these
times. Mike compromised. A Caribbean 'trainer' would be
going to Belize, and he offered to pay to the Ministry of
Defence the cost of extending the flight for the journey from
Belize to Lima and return.

'I must be the first serving R.A.F. Officer ever to charter an
R.A.F. Hercules,' he wryly claimed.

By January 1982 there were 160 applications from Service
personnel for membership of the expedition. Some of the
applicants were already known to Mike, and he could make a
decision without necessarily seeing them.

Corporal Stuart Forbes, for instance, wrote from R.A.F.
Germany. As a member of the Nepal expedition, Yorkshire-
bred Stuart had been selected for his versatile engineering
skills. Knowing that the easy-going Stuart could work in harmony with any group of people, Mike selected him for Peru, as
a member of the engineering team.

Those who were unknown to either of us were assessed on
the strength of their qualifications and experience, and the
recommendation of their Commanding Officers. Promising
candidates were invited to London to be interviewed by the

31

selection committee – Mike and myself – in January. If they managed to get to the capital on time, from the snow-bound provinces, they had at least shown persistence and initiative.

Time was short, so the successful candidates heard the outcome of their interview immediately. Some were surprised to be taking on team duties almost as they walked out of the door. The commitment expected of them was immediate and concrete. As they left with smiling faces, we told them how they could get to Earl's Court, where we were proudly exhibiting River Rover 03, the first completed Mark 3 craft, in the 1982 Boat Show. Tony Maher and Ingrid, my wife, who shared the task of manning our stand and raising support from other exhibitors, learned who had been selected when they turned up to introduce themselves.

Sub Lieutenant James McClune was just completing his Dartmouth training when he applied for the expedition, and the voice of caution said that he should not be encouraged to take on something outside the mainstream of his career at this stage. Yet this young Christian officer's enthusiasm for the aims of the project, a commitment which we saw as essential, was undeniable. Mike gave him special responsibility for liaison with the missionary organisations in preparation for the Pucallpa phase of the expedition. Going against the trend, James had appeared for interview with a luxuriant Naval beard, but spent his time in the jungle clean-shaven; most of the team did the opposite.

One of Julian's requests for help had been for a boost to the valley's negligible dental facilities, even if only temporarily. Mike interviewed a number of Service dentists for the team. Surgeon Lieutenant Catherine White R.N. brought an impressive history of expedition work as well as her dental expertise. She was also thoroughly prepared for the interview. Did she know the writings of a dental professor famous for his Third World work, asked Mike.

'I have already been to see him,' she replied.

Mike did not doubt that Cathy was worthy of the task, but he was wary of the problems that might arise from a female presence in a male-dominated team. Meanwhile Miss Louise Arrow, an attractive blonde nurse from St. Thomas's Hospital, had been bombarding Mike with pleas to help the medical programme of the expedition.

It had to be two girls, or none, Mike felt. He accepted both, and the presence of Cathy and Louise served to complement the team's masculinity.

Like Louise, some members of the team with special skills to offer came from the civilian world. A friend of Mike Cole, the Rev. Michael Perry, was Chaplain to the Police Staff College, whose Commandant was Sir Kenneth Newman. An idea shared between Sir Kenneth and his Chaplain led to the addition to the team of the considerable talents of Inspector Tim Hollis of the Metropolitan Police.

As the weeks passed, the signs became increasingly encouraging for the project. There has been a long tradition of serving officers leading major British expeditions, most notably Captain Scott (Antarctica 1912) and Colonel John Hunt (Everest 1953). As well as scrutinising and endorsing worthwhile projects, the Joint Services Expedition Trust fosters this tradition by giving to one expedition, every second year, the enhanced 'sponsored' status and a grant from the Trustees of £10,000.

In January 1982 our expedition to Peru was given the eleventh sponsorship, together with the welcome addition to our budget. On February 10th an exhibition was staged to display the achievements of twenty-five years of expeditions supported by J.S.E.T. Mike had the privilege of sharing his plans for Peru with the principal guest, Admiral of the Fleet Sir Terence Lewin, the Chief of Defence Staff. Unknown to either of them, the C.D.S. would all too soon be mounting his own expedition to South America.

Mike received support from other quarters. While serving at the R.A.F. College, Cranwell, early in 1980, he had sought permission to do some dry trials with the River Rover on the college sports field. The Commandant, Air Vice Marshal John Brownlow, agreed – provided that he could try driving it. He had now become Director General of R.A.F. Training, a post controlling Service expedition training. The threads of Divine provision for the hovercraft project always remained strong. At times, though, they were invisible to the human eye: then Mike's faith and patience were severely tested.

The engineering team was led by Royal Naval hovercraft engineer Roy Millington, a staunch member of the Naval Christian Fellowship. The group found themselves put to work rather sooner than they expected: they were dispatched *en masse* to the Isle of Wight workshops of Dodnor Marine Ltd., the builders of the River Rover, to work sixteen hours a day ensuring that the two craft under construction would be ready in time for our deadline.

The strong team of engineers took to the work with determination. Roy was able to draw on considerable River Rover experience. Bruce Vincent, who had just left the R.A.F. as a Chief Technician, had been an engineer in the Nepal team. So had Doug Cooledge, who normally worked with Roy at the R.N. Hovercraft Trials Unit across the water at Lee-on-Solent. Powerful marathon runner Allen Wells was another R.N. engineer. Young Paul Turton too, was a big man, who had earned his place, despite his relative youth and inexperience, because he had been brought up in Peru and spoke fluent Spanish. Chief Technician Dick Ball had spent his childhood with his missionary parents in the Amazonian jungle, and helped meet our urgent need for those who could speak the lingua franca of South America.

Very few of the team gained their places on the grounds of one particular skill. Each member of an expedition has to be able to turn his hand to any task; he (or she) must have, to at least some degree, the knack of working without friction cheek by jowl with those from other backgrounds and possessing different skills. In an environment with no room for prima donnas, the ability to see the humorous side is essential.

One of the last to join the team could be forgiven for not battling his way through the snowdrifts. Sergeant Jim Mudie of the Royal Electrical and Mechanical Engineers wrote his application from a hospital bed, where he was recovering from an operation on the toes of both feet. He carefully described an impressive series of experiences and achievements which would qualify him to be a South American explorer.

'And,' he wrote as he closed, 'I can eat three Shredded Wheat!'

CHAPTER THREE

Moving Target

T HE PLANNED DATE for completion of the two new River Rovers was March 31st, 1982. Non-engineers were drafted in to the Isle of Wight workshop, for two weeks at a time, if they could be spared from their duties. Dentists became skirt stitchers; sailors fashioned plywood decks, in the frenzied bid to meet the target.

In our plans, we had denied ourselves the luxury of a professional photographer, but as the engineering deadline loomed closer and Mike searched for ways of augmenting the team, Stu Antrobus was drafted in. He had an engineering background but was also a Royal Naval photographer.

'While you are down in the workshop,' said Mike to the young Glaswegian, 'you can take some photographs. But I doubt if you will have time!'

So we had gained a photographer.

Later, as our plans to negotiate a TV film of our exploits foundered on the rocks of union rules and film crew first-class fares, Stu found himself learning the complex techniques of film-making. The results were superb, and in fact Stu's film is being prepared for a TV showing.

Elsewhere, too, the tempo was increasing as we rushed headlong into the final weeks of preparation. At R.A.F. Lyneham in Wiltshire, Captain Alan Batty, R.C.T., our logistics member, was amassing an ever-growing mountain of equipment for transport either on our 'chartered' R.A.F. Hercules or by ship.

The final shape of the 28-member team was rapidly becoming

35

clear. The project had benefited from the unusual decision of British Airways to stand down some of their aircrew for several months on full pay. Flight Engineer Mike Duke had undertaken the test-driving programme of our new Mark 3 craft at Dodnor Marine. Now, having been recalled to Heathrow, he took two years' leave entitlement at once to bring his River Rover experience to Peru. Former R.A.F. aerobatic pilot, Squadron Leader Dick Bell, joined us too, as another hovercraft pilot and instructor.

Financially, too, the final threads were being drawn together. Platform guests at the Christian Booksellers' Convention at Blackpool in March 1982 included Dr. Billy Graham, Eurovision Song Contest winner Dana, and Mike Cole, whose book on the Nepal expedition had recently been published. The Convention organiser arranged to borrow the film of the Nepal expedition, and on Wednesday March 3rd, Mike had the opportunity to share our plans for Peru with all the delegates, resulting in large sales of the special edition of *Journey to the Fourth World*, and the swelling of our expedition funds. Each of the team members was handed a quota of books to sell, too.

Encouraged by his special interest in the Third World, and his position as Britain's member of the Brandt Commission, we approached Mr. Edward Heath to ask if he would honour the expedition by becoming its patron. 'Gladly,' was his reply.

Roy's engineers met their deadline, and transported the shiny new machines to Lyneham. The equipment was assembled and ready. The team would meet on April 13th at R.A.F. Brize Norton, near Oxford, for final briefing and last-minute inoculations. A valedictory meeting of sponsors and supporters would take place on the 19th. All was prepared.

The Royal occasion was planned for May 3rd, 1982. Peru's Banco Continental had offered to stage the hovercraft display for Princess Alexandra in the foyer of their prestigious headquarters in Lima – and to make a generous donation to the expedition. Riding high, Mike broke his hectic U.K. schedule on April 1st to fly to Lima and finalise the arrangements for the Royal visit.

A few hours after landing, he heard the news.

'Argentinian Dawn Attack.' The British Embassy was buzzing with reports of the invasion of the Falkland Islands by Argentinian troops at six a.m. on April 2nd. After a fierce battle in which three Argentinians were killed, the seventy-nine Royal Marines defending Port Stanley had been ordered by the Governor to surrender. Outside the Argentinian Embassy in Lima, the traffic lights had stuck on red, symbolising to Mike the sudden barrier to the expedition.

Mike agreed to honour his commitment to speak on Peruvian breakfast television, provided that there would be no political content. Nevertheless, he was asked the inevitable question.

'What about the Malvinas?'

'I can only trust,' he replied carefully, 'that the developing crisis will not prevent our helping those isolated Indian people who have never heard of the Malvinas or the Falklands.'

The Royal plans in abeyance, Mike flew home with a heavy heart. But by the time he arrived at the Brize Norton meeting he had regained some of his optimism. The task force, bristling with military power, had sailed from the Solent on the 5th. South Georgia had been taken by the Argentinians, but as yet there had been no major losses on either side. Alexander Haig, the American Secretary of State, shuttled between London and Buenos Aires seeking to bring the two sides together. It seemed at least possible, as the task force made its slow but resolute progress southwards, that disaster might be averted.

The uncertain team that met at Brize Norton on April 13th was not constituted exactly as had been planned. Surgeon Lieutenants Andy Prosser, Cathy's dental partner, and Ross Adley, the team's R.N. doctor, were southbound on a luxury liner, with the fleet. Other members had suddenly been called to other pressing duties. Tony Maher was still with us, having heard with disgust that his Royal Marines unit had left without recalling him. He spent days searching for a way of catching up with them.

'If you let him, he'll swim to Port Stanley,' I commented to Mike.

A telephone call brought the final blow. Mike read out the message from the Defence Attaché in Lima.

'FALKLANDS CRISIS AND INCREASED TERROR-IST ACTIVITY IN AYACUCHO REGION MEAN WE MUST RECOMMEND INDEFINITE POSTPONE-MENT.'

It was a devastating setback to the months of preparation. In a characteristic act of faith, Mike asked the doctors to carry on with the administration of inoculations to the dejected team members.

The loss of Ross Adley and Andy Prosser to the task force had left the essential medical team severely depleted. To augment it, Mike looked outside the Services. Dr. Bill Gould, the missionary doctor whose fertile imagination had originated the 'hovering doctor' concept, had now returned from Nepal to a general practice in Brixham, Devon. He and his three partners had previously agreed to act as expedition medical officers, one by one, on a 'rota' basis. After the Falklands Crisis they employed a locum for their practice at their own expense, to ensure that we would still have two doctors at any one time.

Throughout the growing crisis that summer, Mike Cole had an inner conviction that the expedition should go forward. Understandably, the feeling was not shared by many. Friends commiserated, acquaintances nodded knowingly. However, Mike's boss, Group Captain Peter Hearn, reasoned that in the aftermath of the crisis there would be a need to restore good Anglo-Latin American relations. He encouraged his energetic subordinate not to give up.

Nevertheless, the valedictory meeting on April 19th would have to be postponed until prospects for the expedition were more definite. Mike delegated to me the heartbreaking task of going through the file of accepted invitations, and phoning through the postponement. That file of names represented months or even years of his efforts to gain support. We prayed that the support would not be permanently lost.

All who had bought books, or the First Day Covers that said we were departing on May 1st; all who prayed for our success – they were all important. The First Day Covers, like our expedition sweaters, were embellished with our expedition symbols, a stylised condor and humming bird, copied from the gigantic 1500-year-old designs on the desert plain of Nazca.

Nobody knew why the design existed – my favourite theory involved ancient hot-air ballooning – but the symbols had seemed appropriate when Mike and I had first visited Peru. The condor, gliding effortlessly over the snow-capped Andes, is often thought of as a symbol of the mountain Indians in their struggle for survival. The humming-bird, or *picaflor*, has no such pretensions; but, like River Rover, it hovers.

On April 16th, another signal arrived, a testimony to Captain Malcolm Carver's continued efforts to salvage something from the Peruvian Foreign Office.

'BRITISH JOINT SERVICES EXPEDITION NOT POSSIBLE, BUT SMALL GROUP ON TECHNICAL CO-OPERATION BASIS MIGHT BE ACCEPTABLE.'

But the South Atlantic crisis deepened, with no sign of a solution.

Tony Maher, in the London office, tried to get in touch with Ian Mather and Tony Prime, the *Observer* reporter and photographer who had planned to cover our exploits for their paper.

'Last time I heard from them, they were in Buenos Aires,' said the News Editor. Later we heard that they had been arrested as spies in the Argentinian port of Punta Delgado.

The hovercraft and other equipment were moved to Liverpool Docks, to be loaded on to the Chilean-owned, Liberian-registered, Hong Kong-managed, Indian-captained, and Filipino-crewed S.S. *Rubens*, bound for Lima. In view of the uncertainties on the Latin continent, Mike asked Alan Batty and Flight Lieutenant Ernie Clark of the R.A.F. Regiment, who had responsibility for our jungle equipment, to accompany the consignment. To our relief, the ship got under way safely as the situation in the South Atlantic became more tense.

During their slow progress across the grey and sombre Atlantic, they started to pick up snippets of news from the South and took to spending much time in the radio cabin. As the situation grew worse, they heard from Mike the alarming news that the Lima dockers were refusing to handle British cargo. With this in mind, as *Rubens* passed at night through the brightly-lit Panama canal, Ernie and Alan clambered down into the hold to delete any English markings and ensure that our equipment was clearly marked in Spanish with the name of its recipient *Fundacion Amazonica* (Amazon Trust).

Concern had grown in Lima at the thought of two British military officers arriving at the height of the tension. Lima newspapers were already publishing vitriolic attacks on Britain. Mike had instructed the pair to leave the *Rubens* at the Ecuadorian port of Guayaquil if they did not hear otherwise, and with the crisis worsening, rather than improving as he had hoped, he could not allow them to proceed to the Peruvian capital. The pair left the ship at Guayaquil and returned home sadly to a country at war.

In their absence, the signs from the turbulent South had become less and less hopeful. While much of Latin America came down firmly on the side of Argentina, the United States made enemies in her neighbouring continent by supporting Britain.

We watched for indications of where Peru would place her allegiance. The reports were confused. In the Apurímac valley, where the riverside clinics awaited us, a strong measure of support for Britain testified to the goodwill Julian had gained. In the capital, the media were fiercely, crazily anti-British. The Peruvian military had close links with Argentina – the Army's top General had trained there – and there were rumours that Peruvian jets had already been sent to Argentinian bases. In the centre, President Fernando Belaúnde Terry's civilian government tried to adopt a neutral stance while looking over its shoulder at the military; the President proposed a seven-point peace plan to bring the Argentinian junta around the table with Mrs. Thatcher. But hopes were fading as attitudes in Buenos Aires hardened.

On May 2nd another signal arrived from Lima:
'ALL NEGOTIATIONS ON EXPEDITION ARE IN SUSPENSION.'

On May 3rd the *General Belgrano*, the second largest ship in the Argentinian fleet, was hit and sunk by a British submarine.

Despite the efforts of the Peruvian Secretary-General of the United Nations, Xavier Perez de Cuellar, all hope of a peaceful solution now seemed lost. On May 22nd, a British bridgehead was established on East Falkland.

The British people gathered tensely around their television sets every evening to hear the latest news, as their forebears had gathered around the radio in the 1940s. Ministry of Defence spokesman, Ian Macdonald, became a new TV celebrity, his slow, careful voice a fascinating counterpoint to the frenetic outbursts and unfounded claims that issued from Buenos Aires.

H.M.S. *Ardent* sunk; H.M.S. *Coventry* bombed; Goose Green recaptured; R.F.A.s *Sir Galahad* and *Sir Tristram* damaged; Bluff Cove retaken. With each new despatch, I shared the feelings of my neighbours and friends. Relief at the successes; sadness for the losses; pride in my professional colleagues. Yet superimposed on these feelings was a powerless frustration. Every shot fired seemed to take the prospects for our expedition further into a dream world.

But if our plans were to come to nothing, what of the months of preparation? For years past, we had felt that God's hand had been on the project, guiding and driving us forward. There *was* a purpose in what we had been doing, I decided, and I would not accept that our work would be wasted.

On June 14th, 1982, the routed Argentinian conscripts fled before advancing British soldiers from the high ground overlooking Port Stanley, throwing down their weapons as they ran. That night, at one minute to midnight, General Mario Menendez signed a surrender document on behalf of his 12,000 occupation troops. Four weeks of tragedy and triumph were over.

Three weeks later, Mike telephoned Kit Marshall, a Lima businessman who had lent his enthusiastic support to the expedition's cause, to take the pulse of developments in the Peruvian capital.

'What about the Argentinian crisis?' he asked.

'They are taking it very badly here,' replied Kit, 'especially the disputed penalty for the third goal.' The World Cup had taken over completely in Latin America.

Many of the team had given up believing that the expedition would take place in the near future, if at all. Not Mike Cole. If such rapid changes of attitude were possible on this volatile continent, he reasoned, then our project might just be able to advance. He optimistically made a provisional booking with British Caledonian Airways for our new low-key technical aid project to leave for Peru on September 2nd, 1982. A small advance party would leave on August 28th.

As Servicemen had to drop out, Mike became more dependent on the civilian members of the newly reorganised team. From the Brixham medical practice, Bill Gould and David Wood were to be our doctors for the first half of the expedition. Halfway through, they would be replaced by the other two partners, the dapper, young-looking David Langley, and Swiss-born Horace Pile, who at fifty-nine would become the senior member of the team.

More or less pessimistic signals came regularly; the expedition was alternately on, then off, then on again. The ground rules for our operation to go ahead changed constantly; we seemed to be trying to hit a running target. The dramatic journey to Pucallpa, the major adventure of the project, came under threat.

'APPROVAL TO GO AHEAD BY NO MEANS CERTAIN,' read the signal on August 10th. 'NO QUESTION OF YOUR EXPLORING 1000 KM DOWNSTREAM. APPROVAL FOR DEPLOYMENT WILL BE FORWARDED WHEN OBTAINED. NOTHING SHOULD BE FINALISED.'

Mike snatched a few days' leave to tone up physically for the coming trials, only to be recalled from the slopes of Ben Nevis as new obstacles confronted our move forward.

Terrorists, who had previously been active only in the mountainous region around Ayacucho, had extended their activities to the capital. Explosions destroyed the power cables that supplied the city's electricity. Later, a bomb was tossed into the gatehouse at the British Ambassador's residence. More uncertainty. The strain told on the families too. The team had to carry on with their normal work, with their bags half-packed for a quick departure.

'I don't like the thought of his going,' said my wife, Ingrid, to Jackie Cole, thinking of the three months' separation, 'but if they have to go, I just wish they could get on with it!'

As the planned departure date approached without any

clearance to move, Mike tried to press for an answer. Despite our deadline, the Defence Attaché could only move with such speed as the Lima bureaucrats would allow him. It is said that if you want someone to arrive on time for an appointment or a party in Peru, you must put on the invitation *hora inglés* (English time). Otherwise they will turn up an hour or so later; that is *hora peruana*, a measure of the Latin attitude to urgency. In South America, 'now' means 'any time today'; 'as soon as possible' means 'any time this week'; and 'immediately' means 'tomorrow'!

Deadlines slipped by. We changed our British Caledonian reservations five times. On the fourth occasion the long-suffering B. Cal. staff made special arrangements to squeeze extra Economy seats into their DC 10 to accommodate us. Becoming more and more embarrassed about the constant changes as our departure date slid back from one flight to the next, Mike delegated the negative telephone calls to the airline to me.

Our expedition would be the first British government involvement in Peru, and probably the first in South America, since the cessation of hostilities. Everyone in Lima, it seemed, had to give his approval, and the Foreign Ministry would not budge until they had the agreement in writing. Not least on the list of signatories was that avowedly pro-Argentinian Army General; to get his signature would be a miracle. It turned out that a friend of Julian's was the General's closest friend; he reassured him about our positive humanitarian intent, and the agreement was given.

Early on September 8th, just twenty-one hours before final postponement would have taken place, and just about the time limit for the team to get to Gatwick, clearance to travel was given. Eighteen eventful weeks late, a second task force was miraculously on its way to South America.

CHAPTER FOUR

Weighing In

'I'M SORRY, MADAM,' said the tartan-clad girl politely, 'but you'll have to pay excess baggage.' The buxom Negress shrugged as she reached inside her voluminous coat for an expensive-looking handbag.

'How much?'

'Gatwick to Lagos for the two extra bags . . . that comes to £496,' announced the hostess. Stunned, I watched the middle-aged Nigerian casually count out nine £50 notes, and the small change. We were next in line, all twenty-two of us, and we had sixty-five items to check in, excluding some very noticeable items of hand baggage. Destination – Lima.

Chris Bunney took charge of checking us in, while Mike Cole stood beside him, casually draping his British Caledonian company tie over the counter. The girl gaped at the overloaded trolleys, piled with rucksacks, suitcases, empty fuel tanks, and coils of aerial wire. If they charged us excess baggage, it would break the bank before we even left London.

Mike explained our close links with the airline to the confused young woman. 'Help,' she cried, and the reservations computer came to the rescue. Next to our oft-changed booking on the screen were the words 'maximum assistance'. Our sixty-nine pieces of luggage disappeared down the chute without a penny changing hands. B. Cal. had done it again.

The DC 10 was full at the start of the eighteen-hour journey, but it became less crowded at each successive stop. Those like Louise, who had the dormouse's ability to sleep anywhere, stretched out on a row of seats and arrived in Lima rested and relaxed – well, almost.

As we stepped with a feeling of dazed unreality on to Peruvian soil, the familiar figure of Julian Latham strode across the tarmac to greet us. If some had not quite believed all this was happening, this was their moment of truth.

Julian brought us up to date as we queued for Immigration. The shipping container of equipment and three hovercraft still languished in Callao, Lima's ocean port, awaiting Customs clearance. I was thinking of the luggage being unloaded at that moment from the DC 10. What would the airport Customs officer think?

When the moment came, our hotch-potch of bags and boxes was cleared with a bored wave of the hand. Only after most of us had walked through did the female Customs officer baulk at a trolley piled high with Johnson fuel tanks; a swift word from Dr. Felix Perez, the Amazon Trust's administrator in Lima, smoothed her ruffled feathers.

'*Buenas noches, mi coronel . . . capitan,*' grinned a familiar Pepe as we climbed into his taxi. On our earlier visit, Mike and I had laughingly accepted the military titles our hosts had thought appropriate. The titles were hard to shake off, but we were trying to reduce the emphasis on our military status.

'No,' laughed Mike, 'call me Miguel.' Pepe gave a puzzled frown, the first of many. As we later started our work in the jungle there were few who thought that 'Don Miguel' – 'Don' is a term of respect for those in a leadership position – and his men were anything other than a military team. The easy-going Indians simply humoured our 'low profile' approach.

Although Lima spends much of its time covered in *la garúa*, the depressing mist which results from the proximity of the cold Humboldt current, the city seems to undergo metamorphosis when the sun breaks through. The broad palm-lined avenues and colonial architecture evoke the atmosphere of Andalusian Spain. Despite Lima's 12°S Latitude, and its desert surroundings, though, the constant grey skies are the norm. Indeed, *limeños* joke that the conquering Pizarro chose the site on the malevolent advice of the subjugated Incas.

After a very short night's sleep, the team set to work in Lima. Mike discussed our plans with the new Defence Attaché, Captain Don Ross R.N., while the team were briefed by

Embassy staff on local conditions; without obsessive precautions we could expect to lose camera, wristwatch and passport to the slick thieves who work the streets. The engineers inspected the hovercraft at Callao. Cathy visited a snake farm to obtain anti-venom serum ready for our coming experiences; if some-one is bitten, she was told, the most important thing to do is catch and identify the snake!

On Sunday morning a number of us attended an English-language church service, where Mike and Bill described something of our plans and Chris, the team treasurer, sold several copies of *Journey to the Fourth World*. I suppose that the Church of the Good Shepherd is a Cathedral Church because it is the home of the Anglican Bishop of Peru, David Evans. But it doesn't look like a cathedral and neither does it much resemble a typical South American church. In appearance it is a normal suburban Anglican church in the modern style, transplanted as a unit into South America. As one might expect, it serves the sizeable British community in the capital. But the church also has a large Spanish-speaking membership and holds Spanish services. Inside, the illusion of being in Banstead or Godalming is not shattered. Jackets and ties are the order of the day. Nevertheless, the church has a warmth and a welcoming atmosphere, and its members showed a great interest in our mission.

At the church, Mike and I renewed an old acquaintance. On our previous visit in June 1981, I had been asked by my uncle to look up two missionaries who were supported by his church. The task had expanded, and I had carried family gifts for this couple, who worked among the people of the suburbs and slums of the city, running a leather craft workshop for unemployed young men. Steve and Diane Lee were a young Yorkshire couple with three small children, who somehow seemed too 'normal' to fit into a missionary 'image'. In 1981 I had brought several items sent by Steve's father, including a small parcel of sweets and chocolate which the family would have to eke out for several months to come. The involvement of the Lee family with our project was to last a good deal longer than that parcel of sweets. Even though the team bought quantities of the Lee's leather goods, I often wondered who gained the most benefit, for their house became our expedition 'hotel' as various members passed through the capital.

Steve also found himself pressed into service as a tour guide.

'You've seen the prosperous city centre,' Mike told the team. 'Now I want you to see the other side of Lima.'

As we approached some of the more recent additions to the city and gazed at the rows of dust-covered hovels, Steve explained how these 'young villages' develop. When an Indian comes down from the mountains in search of work he will probably build himself some kind of simple shelter in one of these areas, made up of four walls of straw matting. There may be a roof, or there may not. It doesn't really matter because the rain, in Lima, only comes about once in every ten years. If the search for employment is successful, then the newcomers may move on to the next stage of construction. The inhabitants of one particular area would probably get together, as a community or co-operative, and start to build their own houses, using concrete or bricks, and eventually own a more permanent structure. As building progresses a *de facto* housing estate starts to develop. It is at this stage, perhaps after several years, that the Government may step in. After coming to some financial agreement with the leaders of the new community, it may agree to install a water supply of some kind, and perhaps even electricity to the buildings.

Life is hard in these slum dwellings on the desert hills around the city of Lima, a total contrast from the chic high-class suburbs, Miraflores and San Isidro. But the inhabitants obviously feel that life is even harder back in their mountain villages.

The dry desert atmosphere ensures that the hillsides present a dismal picture to those who look up at them from the city. It is said that when Charles de Gaulle, as President of France, visited Peru in the days of the military regime, the city authorities were worried about the impression given by the slums. They set the painters to work. Soon, from a distance, neat white dwellings glistened in the sunlight, but it was obvious when walking among the buildings that only the side facing the city had been painted. Under the white façade the dirt and squalor were still there.

47

Although President Belaunde's government had been elected in 1980, making Peru, arguably, the only truly democratic country in the whole continent, it is difficult for Peru to cling to the threads of democracy after years of military dictatorship. We, who have hundreds of years of parliamentary heritage, find it hard to understand how South American countries can have such difficulty in sustaining the democratic habit.

Interwoven with the complex web of politics and power in the country was another factor – the Church. Roman Catholicism, in one form or another, is still the religion of the majority of the population of South America. We learnt that, in Peru, it had three strands. The traditional movement was inextricably linked with the existing hierarchy. What might be called the Liberation Movement was the Church's reaction to the overwhelming poverty that prevailed throughout the continent. The third strand, the Charismatic Movement, was probably the one with the closest links with churches outside Roman Catholicism. We were surprised how recent, in some parts of South America, was the freedom for these Protestant churches to exist openly at all. And yet this small minority was growing.

Where was the growth concentrated? Was it among the smart city set, or in the middle-class professional group? No. The major growth was taking place among the poor in the shanty towns on the edge of the city, and in the rugged mountains. Maybe men have to reach rock-bottom before being willing to hear about God.

Our mission was inextricably linked with the shanty-towns of Lima's dusty hills. If the mountain or jungle villagers could be sure of a little security back home, they would not find the deceptive attractions of the city so irresistible. We were here to boost Julian's work, and Julian was dedicated to making his own small corner of Peru more habitable.

That had not always been his aim. The story behind his fourteen years in Peru had moved us all, increasing our determination that the project should succeed.

When Julian had left his farm in Rhodesia in 1965, the year of Ian Smith's U.D.I., he had no clear plan other than to get out of a country whose direction he could not agree with. He

Amazon River

The Team

San Francisco welcomes the team

Unloading River Rover

Launch at San Francisco   A bellyful of worms

Wheelbarrow ambulance makes it to the clinic

Conquering the headwaters

had drifted around England, now working on a North Sea gas platform, now in London as a mini-cab driver or on the upkeep of the capital's parks.

Then in 1967 he met Father Ford, the Rector of the Roman Catholic school in Salisbury where Julian had been a pupil.

'What are you doing now, Julian?' asked the priest, after talking over the past and casually recounting the changes in the new Zimbabwe.

Julian laughed. 'Oh, tidying up London and keeping the flowers going.'

'How would you like to go to Peru?'

'Peru?' Julian was startled. 'What's there to do in Peru?'

Father Ford laughed at Julian's reaction. Then he became serious.

'The Benedictines have a Mission out on the other side of the Andes, a farming project that isn't going very well. You are an agriculturalist, and they need someone out there for a year to help sort it out.'

Julian was sceptical. He had no great interest in South America, and he certainly did not feel at home when Father Ford persuaded him to visit the Benedictine monastery in England, with its forbidding iron-studded doors and noiseless monks. The Abbot gently explained their need.

'Our Brothers out in Pichari have been struggling,' he said. 'We felt it right to start the agricultural work because we needed to *do* something in that part of the world, so that our preaching would have some practical outworking. We saw that the local Indian farmers knew nothing about crop rotation, nor about how much the land needed to be re-plenished to continue to give a good yield. All they did was burn down the forest, steal all the goodness out of it, and then move on and rape another patch of good earth. We felt that our Western technology could be of immense value to them, enabling them to set up permanent homes and farms, thus giving them a stable income from which they could improve their lives. But we have found a number of difficulties. The land has been so drained of its goodness by the forest that it needs a few years to recover its nitrates and potassium and other chemicals. So far, our yields have not been significantly

49

different from those of the local farmers. We need an expert to go out and help us.'

Julian was far from convinced. South American farming would be very different from the African farming that he knew, he explained, and his knowledge of crops was limited to sugar and citrus fruit.

'That's just the sort of expertise we need,' said the Abbot, 'and you know much more about tropical farming than any of us.'

Julian was running out of arguments.

'Where would I live?' he asked slowly.

'In the monastery with the Brothers,' replied the sympathetic Abbot. 'I'm afraid it's rather rough. And I can't offer you any money. We would prefer you to go out there for a year; any less would not be worth the cost of sending you. But,' he continued with a twinkle in his eye, 'we would pay your fare out and back.'

Julian was quiet. He had no great missionary calling, to give away a year of his life in a distant continent. But then the Abbot showed him a photograph of a man he recognised, a priest who had shown kindness to Julian's father just before his death.

'He is my brother.' The Abbot spoke softly, and Julian instantly felt a bond with him. Julian felt as if God was gently pushing him in an inevitable direction.

'I'll go,' he said.

Julian Latham spent his year in the Benedictine monastery at Pichari in the Apurímac valley. But the monks did not have much more success than the indigenous farmers. To improve the yields appreciably, they would need either good fertilisers, which would be almost unobtainable on the wrong side of the Peruvian Andes, or crop rotation. Crop rotation was preferable, but years would be needed before any improvement would show. The time would be better spent in persuading the local farmers to introduce crop rotation themselves. The monks, with Julian's advice, reluctantly wound up the project, and moved out to help the local farmers on an itinerant basis. Julian was free to go home. He had learned a great deal about Peru, and also about poverty and inequality.

'Poverty is a way of life,' he later commented to us. 'It isn't just being poor – not having material things. It's ignorance, and not knowing what things to have. It's a way of life that permeates the whole fibre of your being.'

Working at the Mission was a lad named Armando. Julian had befriended him and taken him on many of his journeys up and down the river. Armando often talked about his family, and was very keen to introduce Julian to them. His fifteen-year-old brother, Mario, had already taken to drink, to drown the traumatic memory of their father's death.

'Let me tell you about when I first arrived at Mario's house,' explained Julian. 'It was made of a few rusted corrugated-iron sheets. I don't know where they had got it from; just picked it up from the rubbish tip, I think. But it was full of holes. Mario and Alfonso (another brother) were there, two little boys and a girl, and five-month-old twins starving to death. Their father had recently died. Their mother was lying on the floor on a sack in the corner, dying of T.B. It started raining, and the water just poured in. We all stood in the corners. There was nothing we could do about the mother, except put a plastic sheet over the top of her. It poured all night, torrential tropical rain coming down in buckets. It was absolutely awful. I thought to myself, "What is going on in the world today?", and I wept.'

A few weeks before Julian was due to go home, a new visitor appeared at the market town of San Francisco. British explorer John Ridgway intended to travel down the Amazon on a balsa raft, and he invited Julian to go with him. With nothing to lose, Julian accepted. They were sucked in by whirlpools, stranded on an island, rescued by Campa Indians – but through all their adventures, Julian was unable to get the unfortunate family out of his mind. The baby twins had died; the mother had succumbed to her tuberculosis, and was dead too. The six orphaned children, with Mario at their head, were left to the ravages of a violent world.

Julian left Ridgway at the jungle city of Iquitos and returned to Lima. There he sold his London air ticket back to the airline and – having burned his boats – returned to the friendless orphans.

The air-ticket money paid for some corrugated iron, some timber and some nails. Julian built a tiny shelter which would serve as a shop and a home for himself and his new charges.

Armando and Alfonso could work in the shop, whilst Mario, who had been taught as a boatman by his father, would be the ferryman between San Francisco and the opposite bank; in those days there was no bridge.

The whole family slept on the floor of the shop, including Julian.

'Sometimes I was worried that I had lost my mind,' he says as he describes those days. 'We were living in poverty. I went around barefoot – I just didn't have enough money to buy shoes. We had enough money to send the children to school and to clothe them for it, but hardly enough to buy food to eat. Yet I felt I was doing something that I really enjoyed. Somehow it all felt right. I can't really tell you why. You can look at it from the point of view of faith. But in the terms of the person in the street, I would say that I felt that was what I was supposed to do in my life. That was why I found such satisfaction in it.'

As a means of support, the shop was not a success. They could barely afford to buy stock for the meagre shelves. What is more, Julian's 'orphans' started to grow in number. Other parents died, and the pathetic little mites would shyly approach him. How could he refuse them? But where could he house them?

As he pondered over the problem of finance, his mind turned to the farmers. Often, he had seethed with anger over the corruption of the San Francisco merchants, who lined their own pockets at the expense of the poor *campesinos*. Julian wondered how he could help the farmers to bypass the merchants; transport was the problem, and the river was their 'road'. If the farmers had their own boats, they could carry their own produce, but the tiny dug-outs and balsa rafts were no use.

Then he remembered a sketch he had seen. It had been an Inca canoe, long and with steep sides to keep the water out in the rapids. Perhaps they could make one. He enquired from local boatmen what wood they used. It was the giant *torneillo* tree, its wood tough and light, long and straight. Julian borrowed a chain saw from a friend, took his six little children, and went to find the tree.

They walked 40 kilometres into the jungle before they found

the right tree. They sawed it down, cut off its branches, cut it in half, and shaped it. Then they hollowed it out by hand. It was March, the rainy season. They had no waterproofs; only the clothes they stood up in. They had no food; they lived on jungle berries, fruit and root crops. They had no shelter, and slept on the rain-sodden earth under a gaping umbrella of Amazonian trees. They worked for six weeks, till their hands were black, their backs were sore, their clothes were torn, and their bare feet massacred by the thorns and ants. When they had hollowed out the base, Julian befriended some local Campa Indians, who helped to carry it to the river. It was 15 metres long.

At a rudimentary sawmill close by, Julian borrowed simple equipment and built the boat's sides. Once they had paddled it down the river to San Francisco, they were able to sell the canoe for the equivalent of £100. A second boat followed and was also sold. The third they kept, and used the money as a down-payment on an outboard motor. They were now equipped as boatmen.

Julian went to the farmers, one by one, and suggested they formed a co-operative. He would transport their produce, at a rate that was more than fair, to wherever they could find a market. Few of the *campesinos* joined in at first, but as the word spread that the offer was genuine, the co-operative grew. By his catalytic action, Julian had brought about a quantum jump in the farmers' fight against poverty.

He had not done it without making enemies. As he challenged the status quo in the valley, exposing corrupt practices, the smarting merchants kicked back. Julian's orphan boys were abused and sneered at in the streets; passers-by spat at them, calling them '*gringo* kids'. The family's boats were cut loose, and outboard motors stolen. Taking advantage of the corruptness of local officials, Julian's enemies had him arrested on three occasions. Ironically, the avid opposition was preventing Julian from doing something about the other concern which burned in his compassionate heart – health. There was no medicine in the valley to speak of. In San Francisco there was a tiny hospital, but it was dilapidated and unused. There were no doctors, and the life expectancy of the local farmers was forty-five years. Although the co-operatives were growing and multiplying, nothing was being done about health: Julian's attempts to get permission to re-open the hospital had all been blocked.

Under the threat of deportation by the corrupt local officials, he looked for help. Years before, he had been given a letter of introduction to an Archbishop in Lima, himself a man who had seen the inside of a gaol on account of his active defence of the poor.

Julian found the Archbishop to be a very pleasant and sympathetic man, who listened to his story briefly.

'What you need to do is to go and see General Marin, and tell him everything. I'm going to see him tomorrow, and will arrange an introduction.'

General Marin was then eighty-three. He was respected as one of the few genuine and incorruptible men in Peru. It was he who had inaugurated the Military Academy, and had been the driving force behind many reforms in the nation. He had retired from Government and military service, but he still had the ear of every one of the ruling junta.

'I'm an old man,' he said to Julian after a few polite words of introduction. 'And I have all the time in the world. Sit down. Take your time. Tell me everything.'

It took Julian two hours. When he had finished, the grand old man said, 'Let me repeat it back to you, just so that I've got it right. Please correct me if there is anything wrong.' Two hours later, having repeated Julian's story word-perfect, the General said that he would speak to the President about it.

'Leave it with me,' he said, as they shook hands at the door. 'You won't have any trouble from now on.'

From that moment on, Julian's work received the official blessing of the Government from the President downwards. It was the breakthrough that he so desperately needed.

Over the years, Julian had been unable to turn away the impoverished orphans who turned up at his makeshift home. Those who came, he took into his extended family. He managed to find people in Britain who were willing to support the children, especially a dedicated Bristol businessman named Martin Appleby, who helped him by setting up a trust fund.

The Amazon Trust, as it became known, aimed at first only

to help the children, and to date over ninety orphans have
joined the 'family'. As the early members have grown up and
married, they have taken in others. Today there are still forty-
three children of school age living with families rather than in
squalor.

Later, though, as the way opened for Julian to concentrate
on the health of the valley people, the Trust undertook to back
him up with funds. They had some sources – business people,
charities – but Martin also approached the Overseas Development Administration, convincing them that the work was an
excellent advertisement for British goodwill and expertise.
The O.D.A. agreed to pay half of the cost of the health project.

Julian received permission to re-open the San Francisco
hospital in 1978, and quickly turned it into a working hospital.
As soon as it was securely under way, the Trust handed it over
to the Peruvian Ministry of Health, and Julian turned his mind
to the installation of village health posts up and down the valley.
To ensure that the health posts were a success was the purpose
of our journey.

With each successive stage, the weight of our luggage played
an increasing role in our progress towards the jungle. As our
fleet of cavernous black taxis sagged on to their springs at
five a.m. on Monday for the ride to Lima airport, we knew that
the Fokker F.28 to Ayacucho might be somewhat easier to
overload than a DC 10. The six taxis, spirited out of the
darkness by Pepe – 'This is my brother, this is the husband of
my sister, etc.' – made us look like a convoy of Mafiosi as we
bumped along the potholed road.

With an encouraging regard for passenger confidence, the
stewardess crossed herself just before take-off, but we arrived
in the Andean township safely after the thirty-minute flight,
and with our luggage relatively intact. Of the eighty-six items
checked in at Lima, only nineteen were missing. When would
they arrive. *Mañana*.

'We are now in the centre of the terrorist area,' proclaimed
Julian as we gathered around our bags in the deserted airport
terminal at Ayacucho. 'I don't think we will have any trouble. I
think they accept that we are only here to help the people.'

The attacks on outlying police posts and desolate mountain telegraph stations had started about three years earlier. The guerillas call themselves the *Sendero Luminoso*, or 'Shining Path', and are so far out on the Maoist left that they accuse Havana and Peking of revisionism. The fanatical *senderistas*, claiming to speak for the Andean peasants, are dedicated to the overthrow of the Lima government; sadly, if they were to succeed, it would probably achieve only the return of military government. The terrorists are a force of destruction and bitter resentment against the country's small percentage of whites and *mestizos*, who have dominated the economy since the Spanish conquest. We hoped to steer clear of them.

'The people here say that the terrorist flag is flying at Tambo,' continued Julian, referring to a village half-way along the dusty road to San Francisco. 'Just to be on the safe side, I'll try to get a light plane to fly you all down to the valley.'

Three hours later, after a price negotiation by radio, a single-engined Cessna 206 approached and touched down on the tarmac runway. Its short, dark-haired pilot, introduced as Miguel, had a casual air as he worked out the take-off weight on his calculator wristwatch.

'There are six seats, but I can't put in more than 400 kilograms,' he announced, apparently satisfied.

In the first group of passengers, I cringed as the stall-warning blared out on take-off – and kept sounding as the little plane sank out of our comrades' sight into the dip beyond the end of the runway. For later flights the shaken Miguel dropped his limit to 350 kilograms.

Half an hour after struggling into the air, the Cessna started to lose height, and below us we saw the girder bridge surrounded by a cluster of dilapidated shanties that was San Francisco. A welcoming speech of the appropriate length, a bouquet of jungle flowers, a kiss from a buxom lovely who was presumably 'Miss San Francisco', and we felt we had arrived. Two grinning children held up a carefully-fashioned banner bearing a heart-warming greeting in English:

'WELCOME TO MICHAEL COLE, P. DIXON AND OUR ENGINEER FRIENDS.'

CHAPTER FIVE

The Great Speaker

T HE BUSTLING, BANNER-WAVING crowd escorted us
across the metal bridge from the airstrip. At the end of
San Francisco's rutted 'main street' was an impressive concrete
building I did not remember, painted in a clean-looking shade
of sky blue. This was Julian's Operations Centre, built with
£12,000 of O.D.A. money since my previous visit.

We were impressed. An office, a lockable engineers' store, a
fuel store and a pharmacy all led off a spacious open-fronted
garage and workshop area, big enough to house three River
Rovers and a Land Rover. At the back, rooms were still being
built as accommodation for doctors and nurses. Beside the
building, where I could remember only a muddy slope, a broad
concrete slipway led to the water some seven or eight metres
below.

'Does the slipway have to be that long?' asked Roy as he
inspected his new domain.

'Yes,' I replied, 'that's how high the river rises in the rains.'

We were glad that the main rainy season was still a long
way off as we prepared our tented Base Camp next to the
airstrip. The riverside site would not have lasted long in the
wet season.

The neat rows of military tents were soon set up alongside a
large green mess tent. By the time the last of the late-comers
had arrived, the camp was habitable.

'The team will need to work from a strong, secure Base
Camp,' Mike Cole had announced; Chris and Tim had the
task of realising his ideal. The most important aspect was

57

hygiene; if our water supply were unsafe or our camp arrangements unhygienic, then the team would be unable to do anything for the valley.

Drinking water came from the nearest source of clear fast-flowing water, a tributary named the Quimbiri (the Apurímac

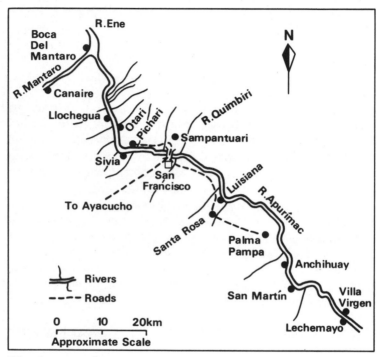

The Apurímac River

itself was a muddy shade of brown). Then it was filtered and chlorinated by a filtration pump. Every few days, someone had to take our stock of jerrycans to the Quimbiri to replenish the 250-gallon storage tank. Even our water for washing was chlorinated, but this came from the main river. Mike instituted a 'recreational' bucket chain on Sundays to ensure that the 2000-gallon inflatable water tank was kept topped up.

The site had been cleared of undergrowth by the Amazon Trust workers before our arrival, mainly to discourage snakes.

We saw few snakes here in the vicinity of the town, although Mike stumbled across one, probably a coral snake, while walking over the riverside boulders at an up-river village. 'Didn't you take a photo of it?' asked his unsympathetic hearers when he returned to the clinic.

Most of the wildlife around the Base Camp consisted of insects of every shape and size. Once Doug Cooledge had installed electric lighting, fed from the tiny Honda generator, the mess tent held a magnetic attraction for the flying nuisances.

'Simple,' laughed Julian, 'paint the bulbs yellow.' We did so, and the insects immediately found other attractions.

Those who slept with their tent flaps open in the tropical heat relied on their mosquito nets for protection, not only against insects but also against the bats which swooped through the tents, leaving their droppings for morning discovery. Most were fruit bats, but some would be vampire bats, transmitting rabies if they bit into the skin. One evening, as I stood motionless at the riverside latrine, I felt a sudden pressure on my shoulder. Startled, I turned and brushed off the shadowy shape of a small bat, which had landed noiselessly on my shirt sleeve. I *think* it was a fruit bat.

Mike insisted on good food, too, and we employed three of Julian's boys to help prepare it. They thrived, as we did, on the combination of military composition ('compo') rations and local vegetables and fruit. Maxi, at thirty-three the oldest, was an open, joyful Christian man who greeted us each morning with grins and handshakes and the Latin embrace – the *abrazo*. He would bring baskets full of papayas or oranges from his *chacra*, his little homestead up the river which he had left in the charge of his wife while he worked in our camp.

Tall, slim Virgilio was more reserved, but the young man was ambitious and full of initiative; always keen to learn English, he would take on any job and complete it without supervision. In contrast, the third worker, a stepson of Maxi's named Boss, had to be pointed to each individual task. One day, for instance, he was given a shovel and told in Tim's expressive sign language to dig a small pit for rubbish; an hour later, when his absence was noticed, he was found in the pit, still digging – all that was

59

visible was an occasional shovel-full of earth flying out of the hole.

Gradually, the camp became more organised; the smooth-running routine was rarely disturbed. We would retire early and rise early, though none so early as 'Don Miguel'. When the leader woke at four or five in the morning, he used to miss the constantly available tea of our Nepali base camp four years earlier. Twice, in his struggles to light the temperamental petrol cookers, he nearly burned down the mess tent; with apologies to C. S. Lewis, I threatened to name this book 'Voyage of the Dawn Fire-raiser'.

The routine involved the different sections of the team in different ways. The engineers had to spend hours in the workshop repairing the damage caused to the hovercraft by their journey across the Andes. When we arrived, only one craft was there. The others followed ten days later, but all had suffered on the rough mountain roads; one truck had even been stuck in a mountain tunnel and the driver had to let the tyres down to budge it.

Even when the initial damage was repaired, the engineers' work was not complete. My initial forays on to the river with the first craft, number 03, resulted in an unexpected landing on a boulder bank which made us realise that the river was not as innocuous as it looked, even close to our base camp. The engineers had already established their collective response, either to a bonus or to a setback.

'Bargain!' said one in a sarcastic tone, and I was *persona non grata* in the workshop for a time.

The main barrier to our progress with the hovercraft, how-ever, was not damage; it was the heat. Even on the River Rover's historic first flight on the Rio Apurímac, driven by Mike Cole, we had not been able to run the craft for more than twenty minutes. Any longer, and the temperature of the water-cooled engine started to rise towards the top limit of 115°C. Wary of using full power on an overheating engine, we found ourselves dropping below the invisible barrier of hump speed (the speed below which the craft is fighting an unequal battle against its own bow wave). We needed to have the full range of power available.

60

Fortunately, the essentially practical engineers on the team were backed up by Dr. Jan Wright, a tall, thoughtful university lecturer in aeronautics from Queen Mary College, London. Jan's trained analytical mind, combined with the practical skills of the other engineers, showed us a way to improve the airflow around the Renault engine and improve the cooling.

When we needed Jan for the engineering work, he was there. As his relatively short stay came to an end, Mike Duke arrived in time to apply his invaluable skills to the hovercraft driving. Yet the two men's itineraries were shaped by totally independent factors. Such things made us recognise the importance of making prayer a regular part of our schedule.

'When we pray, coincidences happen,' said Dr. Stanley Browne, the leprosy doctor who initiated the idea of village health posts and medical auxiliaries. 'When we cease praying, they stop happening.'

Wherever possible, we wanted to involve the Peruvian trainee mechanics of the Amazon Trust in every part of the engineering work, but these problems with River Rover 03 were not conducive to training. However, once we had the two fully-modified craft on the water (05, for the Apurímac, and 06, earmarked for the journey to Pucallpa), 03 was brought into the workshop for its long-awaited engine change and lift-duct modifications. The work was ideal for training the Peruvian mechanics in the construction of the River Rover. The Peruvians watched while one of the team removed some component; later our engineers supervised while the Amazon Trust worker replaced it. If a problem arose, though, it had to be explained – that was when 'Ricardo' was sent for.

With his friendly, easygoing personality and his luxuriant black beard, Dick Ball seemed instantly to endear himself to the people of the town. Having spent his childhood in a similar community, he understood their point of view, and made many friends. 'I am Ricardo,' he would say as the urchin children asked his name, and 'Ricardo' he was universally called.

The engineers, after a day in the grimy workshop, would walk to the clear, bubbling Quimbiri river to bathe; they had resourcefully rigged a rope across the powerful stream for bathers to hang on to, and we came to know the river as the Rio

Jacuzzi. It was the sort of refreshing experience that health clubs sell for a small fortune.

Our constant comings and going became a part of San Francisco's daily life. Even though the Gemini inflatable[1] was used for carrying heavy loads across the river, most of the time we made the short journey on foot. To walk the familiar route from our Base Camp in Teresita to the Operations Centre in San Francisco on the opposite bank was to experience in ten minutes many different facets of the life of the *selva*. The two communities used to be completely separate before the bridge was built, and they still retain something of their separate identities. Indeed, officially, they belong to different Departments, or regions, of Peru.

Stepping through the gap in the fence which insulated us from the outside world, we were immediately in a little crowd of staring children who pressed against the fence, fascinated by the strange ways of the inhabitants of 'Fort Gringo'. It was a boon, though, to have this defined boundary; otherwise we would be overrun by more or less well-meaning invaders.

Reaching the bridge involved picking a way along half the length of the town's airstrip. At one time it had been quite a flat grass surface, but years of misuse by trucks and cars had churned up the mud and left mounds and depressions. It made for a bumpy ride for planes! There were also large areas of standing water to negotiate after rain. To be avoided at any time were the stretches of ground used by the townspeople as public toilets.

A short climb up a rocky bank to the level of the bridge revealed the roadway and civilisation. At either side of the road were tumbledown shacks, most of which were being used for selling something. On market days more and more of the area of the road was covered with goods for sale. The trader would set out his wares on a blanket, and perhaps erect a plastic sheet as an awning against the sun and the rain. When the town was building up to its annual festival the whole length of the bridge was covered with stalls on both sides. The bridge traffic became one-way, and there was more horn blowing to add to

[1]*Gemini inflatable*: inflatable rubber boat used by the Royal Marines, normally with an outboard motor fitted (typical load 4–6 troops).

the cacophony common to markets all over the world, as drivers argued about who would back up.

The bridge was the starting point for transport out of San Francisco. From here a ride could be bought on the back of a truck to Ayacucho or to one of the outlying villages. For a little more comfort, the choice could be one of the small mini-buses which were appearing more and more often as *colectivos*, or shared taxis. Below the bridge on the San Francisco side canoes pulled up at the river bank to discharge their loads of passengers, or of the crops which are the life-blood of the river trade: cocoa, coffee, vegetables and fruit.

Beyond the end of the bridge was the town proper: a town of merchants, with nearly every house doubling as premises for business. Built of concrete, with two or three storeys, each house had an open front on the ground floor which could be closed off by planks or corrugated metal sheets. Straight ahead, steep steps led up to the top end of town, to the banks, the Police Station, and the town's Hotel. At bridge level were the middle-class merchants in simple concrete houses. Down below, close to the water's edge, were the less salubrious houses and shops, mostly wooden shacks, in danger of being swept away whenever the river was in angry spate.

'There is a house in this lower part of the town,' I was told, 'which is in the path of a little stream, but the stream becomes a small torrent in the rainy season. Then the occupants have to evacuate, leaving the front and back doors open, to allow the swelling tributary to make its way down to the main river.'

Whenever we walked between the camp and the workshop there was, inevitably, interest in these strange foreigners. Adults and children alike would call out, shouting '*gringo!*', or 'Good afternoon, meester' (at any time of day) in their best school English. Those who had learned my name would call out '*Buenos dias*, Pedro,' and perhaps grab my hands and walk a short way with me. The call of '*gringo*' or 'white man' sounds like an insult, but the slight was not intended. We were unusual creatures in their town: and our way of dress, pale skin, and preponderance of beards were constant entertainment.

The route to the Operations Centre continued past shops

63

and stalls of every description. Almost anything could be bought – torches and bread rolls, axes and wellington boots – and every third or fourth house was a restaurant. For the outdoor eater there was the spaghetti stall on the small bridge. I suppose it must have seemed as good a location as any. No matter that fifty metres upstream the public toilets discharged their foul effluent into the water.

Further along this 'street', a muddy quagmire after even the slightest rain, was the local butcher's shop. Laid out there would be the choicest cuts of pork or mutton, amid the flies and cockroaches. If there was jointing or slaughtering to be done, a rusty old wheelbarrow served as a chopping table.

The flavour of the town could not be captured merely by the eyes, though. The smells of animals mingled with that of cheap perfume. The delicious odour of smoke wafting from a barbecue stall would be ruined by a whiff of sewage. Noise, too, was constantly in the background. Dogs barked, pigs squealed, truck horns sounded; and from morning to night the loud-hailers blared. There was pop music, and the continual announcements of the next day's events, or of the names of donors to the town's current Appeal.

Each of us would make this short walk one or more times every day. I recall a day when I walked there and back eight times. We naturally became over-accustomed to our surroundings, but every so often a newcomer would point out with amazement some little detail which was no longer visible to the eye of the 'old hand'.

It was not advisable to become over-familiar with the river. 'Apurímac' means 'Great Speaker'; in the high Andes, where the glaciers bleed white water, the river roars like Stentor through the canyon it has carved. But even where we were, the swirling currents could be treacherous, the confused rapids deceptive. We had started the hovercraft driving cautiously, working in the area a few miles up- and down-river and becoming familiar with the rapids immediately above and below our base, before we ventured further afield.

Our aim with the driving was to teach the Peruvians who had been designated as hovercraft pilots, Moises and Aurelio, to handle the craft competently. Former flying instructor Dick

Bell, who already spoke some Spanish, was best suited to that task, and I had stepped back to give him a free hand. But I still held the responsibility for all the hovercraft operations, and I first had to be satisfied that Dick had mastered the vagaries of the river. Dick was impatient to get to grips with the pilot training, and eager to be involved in the decision-making about the expedition. He found my caution and reticence frustrating, but it was not long before I sent him to take his two pupils under his wing.

Of the two, Moises was the more confident. He was a competent car driver, a rarity on the uneven roads of the locality.

'The River Rover will be easy to drive,' he boasted, and in general he proved himself right. Occasionally, though, the hovercraft won, and in the early stages Moises received several jolts to his self-confidence. Aurelio was a more thoughtful, careful pupil; his great strength was his knowledge of the river as a boatman. Once he had mastered the different behaviour of the strange new vehicle, he was very competent.

The work of the team in the valley was proceeding on many fronts. One related to that drunken old man who had chanted 'Carretera Lechemayo'. The road to Lechemayo was held up at the crossing of a small tributary. Encouraged by the O.D.A., who had already provided a metal Bailey bridge for the site, Mike recruited a young graduate civil engineer, Graham Roberts, to survey the area and get the work started. Graham made a detailed survey, carefully investigating the severity of any possible flash flood and assessing whether the river in flood might completely bypass the bridge. His proposal for construction was soon ready, but in the time he had left he was unable to get the materials and labour together to get started. In any case, the period just before the rains was not the time to start such a work. Graham returned home in some frustration, but knowing he had got as far as he could; only the actual construction remained.

It does no good at all to get frustrated in Peru, as Julian had found over the years. The Peruvian, and especially the Quechuan, has a passive personality; if you try to order him about, he smiles and retreats into himself. Sometimes it is difficult to find out the true facts of a situation; the hospitable Indian tells you what he thinks you want to hear.

We had 'settled in' to the valley and we felt secure, but the scent of politics was always there in the background. International affairs were well represented, with 'Malvinas' T-shirts frequently in evidence, but nobody tackled us seriously on that subject. Even if they did, we were under strict instructions from Mike not to enter into discussion.

On the national scale, we were keenly aware that we were in a terrorist area. A few weeks after our arrival, the town was put under curfew from nine p.m. to five a.m. each night, reportedly because the *senderistas* had sent a message to the local judge telling him to resign or face the consequences. The presence of armed police and soldiers became more obvious, and one night a bullet whanged over the Base Camp just above head height.

'Who is shooting at us?' asked Mike angrily of the mayor the next morning.

'Oh, don't worry,' replied the easy-going Peruvian, 'they weren't trying to hit you. They just fire off a few shots to encourage the people to go to bed.'

We became used to the nightly shots just after curfew time, but no more seemed to come our way. Mike kept a tight rein on the team, instructing them to stay out of the local bars and cafes in the evenings, even before nine p.m. The move was understandable: he felt that if we maintained our isolation then we could avoid trouble in the corruption-ridden town. Yet the team had made many daytime friends in San Francisco.

'Why do you keep yourselves locked away?' they asked. 'Are we not good enough for you?'

The ban was unpopular, and when it seemed to have outlived its usefulness I asked Mike to lift it. He refused.

'But some of them are ignoring it,' I said.

'I know,' he replied, 'but at least they will have that feeling of caution in their minds, if they know that the ban still stands.'

Mike also extended our wary approach to Luisiana, and I had to admit that there was sense in that. The Luisiana estate was owned by the influential Señor Pepe Parodi, who had long been a rival of Julian's work in the valley. Indeed, in June 1981

Mike and I had been present when the two men had spoken for the first time in ten years. Yet 'Don Pepe', the area's *diputado* or M.P., also owned the little Cessna, and we had no quarrel with its gregarious pilot, Miguel, who lived at Luisiana. The team had become friends with Miguel and his slim dark-haired wife, but Mike drew the line one Sunday when a few of us visited the estate to share 'Don Pepe's' deserted swimming pool with the couple. With hindsight, perhaps he was right.

Sundays were special days to us. A lie-in until six thirty; a short church service for those who wanted it; maybe an after-noon swim in the 'Rio Jacuzzi' or a game of football on the airstrip against the competent local team. Wherever possible, we reserved Sunday as our rest day, and avoided working, apart from occasional 'recreational' rock-clearing sessions or bucket chains.

One Sunday was different: a major event was planned. October 17th was to be the official hand-over of the *Servicio médico fluvial* from Britain to Peru. The British Ambassador would be coming, with the Peruvian Minister of Health.

On Wednesday, October 13th, plans were progressing smoothly until twelve thirty, when a breathless Julian appeared in the camp.

'The bank has just passed on a radio message,' he panted. 'The Minister can't make it on Sunday; he's postponing the ceremony for ten days. The Embassy want to talk to us direct by radio between twelve thirty and one o'clock.'

Ever since Paul Watson's critical illness, the Embassy had recognised our burning need for direct communications with them, which the government had not permitted. The Ambassador had made a personal plea to the Minister of Telecommunications, and our radio link had been agreed. Although I had sent one of our A.E.L. transceivers to the Embassy, and set up an aerial between my tent and a nearby tree, I had no idea when the link would be established.

The moment had arrived, but the radios were over in the Operations Centre and it was twelve thirty-five already. There was nothing for it: I had to sprint!

Ten minutes there and ten minutes back in the pouring rain; at twelve fifty-six I burst into the tent with a radio which had not been unpacked since leaving the factory, some five months previously. I feverishly attacked the carton; Chris Bunney poked the aerial wires into the back of the set; Stu Antrobus pressed the power cables into the top of a Lucas twelve-volt battery. By twelve fifty-eight we were on the air, and the very English tones of Captain Don Ross answered my tentative call. My worries about my choice of radio equipment before our departure melted away.

We eagerly listened to the news. It was true – the hand-over was postponed until the 27th. Julian sent runners up and down the valley, putting off the teachers and *sanitarios* and village chiefs, some of whom had already left for San Francisco. By Friday, the event had been re-scheduled again. Sunday was on!

On Saturday evening, a cryptic message from Lima created yet more havoc. The official plane, scheduled for ten a.m., would instead arrive at eight a.m. Unsure whether to believe the unlikely tale, we played safe and got up at four forty-five a.m. to prepare the hovercraft and the workshop and camp. We were ready for eight – the plane landed at nine-thirty. Where else but South America could it happen?

There was a slight hitch on our side of things too, however. After the speeches on the Great Day, I took the Ministers of Health and Transport, with the British Ambassador, for a hovercraft ride. After five minutes I noticed a vibration and loss of power. Cautiously putting down on a muddy bank, I caused chaos by depositing the V.I.P.s forty-five minutes early at the Base Camp, where the team were putting the finishing touches to an imaginative buffet luncheon for 120 guests, whose centrepiece was a corned-beef hovercraft.

The temporary hiccup was soon forgotten, but it was only later that the problem was diagnosed. Early that morning, the engineers had hurriedly attached a small object to the side decking of the gleaming River Rover, not realising its precarious hold. It had worked loose and lodged in one of the thrust fans. And what was the mysterious object? A miniature version of the honoured national flag of the *Republica Peruana*.

CHAPTER SIX

By Appointment

'JULIAN'S WITH ME,' said the voice, 'and he wants to speak to Mike urgently.'

Even over the hissing and crackling, with staccato Spanish conversations in the background, the voice was clearly recognisable as David Silver's.

I could imagine the calm, efficient Flight Sergeant sitting in his cool Embassy office overlooking the Lima traffic. Wondering what could be so pressing, I replied that Mike was not with me.

'Stand by,' came the answer. There was a pause, and then Julian's voice filled the tent. Could Mike be brought to the radio as soon as possible? 'It's very urgent . . . it concerns the President.' Even more intrigued, I promised to try, but Mike had just left for the one-hour walk to a vantage point on the other side of the river.

'The situation is this,' continued Julian slowly. 'The President of Peru has asked for the hovercraft to go to Puerto Ocopa. That's approximately 200 kilometres down-river from San Francisco. He has asked that the hovercraft be there the day after tomorrow, Saturday, by eight o'clock in the morning. Over.'

I was thunderstruck. Making a non-committal reply, I agreed to call back at four o'clock: the Minister needed a reply by five.

Mike was helping Stu Antrobus, who wanted to do some filming of the two hovercraft on the river. We had given them one of the A.E.L. radios, but there was no response to our urgent calls to come back. They must have been behind a hill.

A search party was dispatched, but it was nearly two hours before Mike returned and heard Julian's message.

'Impossible,' he said. 'Of course we can't do it.' He thought we meant the next day at eight a.m. In fact we had a full day for the journey, and the rest of us had been working out requirements for time, fuel, food etc. The task was feasible.

Mike Cole called the Embassy while Mike Duke and I took the two hovercraft out for a little 'formation flying' so that Stu Antrobus, who was still patiently waiting up on the hill, would not have wasted a long and heavily laden walk.

Four of us were to set out on the long run down to Puerto Ocopa: Mike Cole, myself and Jim Mudie, together with Stu Antrobus to record what took place. I set about finding the camping kit and food for one or two nights away, and at eight o'clock some of us met for a short prayer meeting to commit the next few days to the Lord.

At eight thirty the next morning, with the back seat bulging with equipment and with two fuel cans strapped to the decks, we were ready for our 'journey into the unknown'. We had 200 kilometres to travel, and no idea of what might await us at Puerto Ocopa.

As we set off from our familiar Base Camp, the overloaded craft sat low in the water. The screaming engine seemed to be at full power for an age before we struggled through hump speed and I could ease back the throttle.

The first hour passed quickly. A continuous series of rapids kept me on my toes as I tried to pick a safe route through the frothing white water, without losing momentum. No longer quite the lively creature we were used to at lighter weights, the machine had to be driven with care, and not a little cunning.

Gradually, matters improved. With every gallon of fuel used, the weight dropped a little. And we were making progress down the river. We passed Sivia and Otari, two of the down-river clinics; the first a bustling market town, the second a simple Campa village. The character of the river was changing. The problem now was not white water, but navigation. Often there was a tantalising choice of routes as the sluggish river split into different channels. In isolated areas of the river we would come across white herons or egrets which would fly

70

up, startled, from the gravel bar which was their territory, or perhaps just turn disdainfully away.

Soon we found ourselves picking our way to the mouth of the Mantaro river, where it joins the Apurímac. The united rivers, now called the Ene, took us on to new territory.

The Ene, for the time being at least, remained easy. In wide sweeping curves it flowed slowly between the jungle slopes. The hovercraft, unlike the canoes, could take short cuts through shallow channels on the inside of bends. In some, the shallows petered out, and we had to retrace our route.

Apart from a brief stop to transfer fuel from jerrycans to the tanks we kept driving on, wanting to get as much distance behind us as possible. It was only after four wearing hours that we reached Quiteni, where it had been suggested that petrol might be available. Quiteni turned out to be a sizeable village; there was petrol for sale at an exorbitant price matched only by the expense of the Coca-Cola! I parked the craft on a bank strewn with driftwood and, amid the fascinated questions of the local boatmen, we bought nine gallons of petrol for the equivalent of £19.

'It's worth it,' said Mike. 'You know what they say about a bird in the hand.'

Onward again. After about twenty minutes the hills started to close in on the river and the flow was constricted into a narrow gorge. I drove on nervously. The flow was strong, and where the river was forced to turn it protested at the intrusion, welling up into great standing waves. In the confused flow downstream of the bend, powerful whirlpools would draw the water downwards. We could not guess at the depth of the river as it poured through the narrowing gorge. At that point I noticed I was suddenly having to use nearly full power just to maintain speed.

We stopped on a bank to see if there was something wrong. Nothing.

'It must be a headwind,' said Jim, but as we stood on the bank there was not a breath of wind. Back to the river, and we were soon using full power again. The needle of the water-temperature gauge flickered to and fro.

'Watch it, Pete, you'll overheat the engine,' called Jim as we

71

puzzled over the mystery. But this time the leaves of the trees at each side showed the gusts of strong wind which were blasting into the front of the hovercraft. I nursed the craft on, balancing the urgency of our pressing appointment against the danger of overheating. Even when the valley widened out the wind barely slackened.

The only solution to the problem was a change of direction and it seemed that it would never come. But at last, six and a quarter driving hours into the trip, we identified the broad opening which had to be the mouth of the River Perene. I turned into it. The change of speed amazed us. Even at low power, we must have been travelling at a comfortable 30 knots.

Less than a quarter of an hour later we saw a river mouth on our left. This, according to our map, was the site of Puerto Ocopa. One of our maps claimed that the place had an airstrip; we thought that might tie in with a Presidential visit.

Behind some coconut palms a few buildings were coming into view. I put the craft down on a muddy bank and we were instantly surrounded by a crowd. As we climbed wearily out of our seats, we were surprised to see two nuns in immaculate white habits, walking down a flight of neat stone steps. Whatever we had expected, it was not this.

What to say? I told them briefly who we were.

'You have visitors to-morrow?' I asked.

'*Si*' said one of them guardedly. The sisters appeared sceptical when I explained about our Presidential summons to bring the hovercraft here for 'inspection'.

The nuns took us up the steps to the buildings while they answered our questions about the place. It was an orphanage, a clinic, a school, run by a Franciscan monk; and yes, the President was expected to visit them in the morning. Mike heaved a sigh of relief. As we walked through the beautifully laid out grounds, and past an imposing chapel, we saw an older man, in a coarse brown habit, working on the engine of an old diesel tractor. His weather-beaten face was lined by years of labour in the hot sun. This was Father Castillo, and he seemed to know something of what we were doing on the Apurímac. He knew Julian, and had known Father Michael for most of the twenty-five years he had been working in the jungle. Puerto Ocopa was his own work.

'Imagine clearing rocks and trees to produce lawns like these,' commented Mike later.

Realising that our throats were parched, two of the nuns took us away for coffee and fruit. As we sat in the cool dining room at a refectory table, eating papaya and not quite believing in this oasis of comfort and calm hospitality, I explained that we did not want to trouble them. We had our own food, but would appreciate some floor space to sleep on. The nuns nodded serenely, and after coffee we were shown to rooms with *real beds* and *real sheets*. Unimaginable luxury.

Later we cooked our rations on stoves outside our rooms.

'Now we'll probably be invited to dinner,' joked Stu. Just as we were ready to wash up the mess tins, a young man came looking for us. 'Come and eat,' he said.

We sat down at the table with Father Castillo and two young men (the nuns and girls ate in a separate room) and we didn't have too much difficulty in getting through the simple but delicious meal of chicken soup, rice with vegetables, and fruit. Only Stu, who had taken full advantage of the compo meal, was defeated. Next morning, he felt very ill, but it did not stop Mike dragging him out to photograph the magnificent sunrise at five a.m.

'Thanks a lot, Mike,' said Stu rather sullenly. Weeks later, when he saw the prints, he said it with more sincerity.

After a novel breakfast of cold fish and yucca, we washed the hovercraft and ourselves, and put on the semi-respectable clothes we had brought with us.

A little parade of school children was formed up and the Peruvian national anthem was sung while the flag was raised. The parade was then marched to the airstrip to wait for the great man's arrival. Not long after nine, one of the local soldiers said he could hear the President's Buffalo[1]. He rushed off to tell the Sisters while we strained to hear any sound. A few minutes later the sand-coloured Buffalo appeared over the mountains,

[1]*Buffalo*: twin-engined light military transport plane, especially useful in remote areas, as it can land and take off in a very short distance on a rough surface.

circled once and made its unbelievably steep approach to the neat grass strip. First out was the TV cameraman. Then President Fernando Belaúnde Terry stepped out on to the turf with a wave, while the little crowd applauded. With his hand the smiling politician smoothed back his grey-white hair; then, with eyes half closed against the bright sunlight, he looked round the onlookers gathered to welcome him.

He was not the stereotype of a South American President. Well built and of medium height, in his light open-necked shirt he exuded an air of fatherly informality. His slightly faltering step betrayed his advancing years. But a keen and confident intellect shone from the clear, piercing eyes. This was the man who returned from exile to lead Peru on its new tentative venture into democracy. '*El Arquitecto*' they called him, after his former profession. He has a burning ambition to build up his country to prosperity; for Peru has vast natural resources, as yet untapped.

He was introduced to Father Castillo. The two men were natives of the beautiful city of Arequipa, but they had much else in common. Castillo too was a dedicated and creative builder. As he stood amidst the products of his toil, in his simple habit, talking quietly to his nation's leader, one could sense that their respect was mutual.

We stood in the background, not wishing to intrude. The British Ambassador stepped out of the plane, searching the faces in the crowd. Espying Mike, he rushed over in relief. Without real conviction, he had assured the President we would be there. The President inspected the small guard of honour and the rows of children, but then impatiently asked where the hovercraft was. He was persuaded to continue with the tour of the Mission and its model Campa village. He gave a short speech of admiration for the work of the Franciscans in the jungle. But then, with the TV camera rolling, he called the Ambassador forward. 'My good friend,' he called him, and described how the British Government had given the hover-craft and other equipment and how we started the medical service in the Apurímac valley. He beckoned Mike and myself over.

Showing the cameraman exactly where he was to stand, the

President of Peru heaped praise on our project for the Channel 7 evening news, in the year when all South America was talking about *Las Malvinas*.

After visiting the Mission primary school, President Belaúnde made it clear that now was the time to see the hovercraft. We walked down the steps to the riverside, the nuns bemused by the bustling pace of the visit. Before climbing into the River Rover with me, the President talked again to the camera about British help and new technology, and the problems of communication in the jungle. In the back of the River Rover sat the British Ambassador, Charles Wallace. 'At least you are not carrying flags this time,' murmured the Ambassador, sotto voce.

The President was fascinated by the sensation of hovering over the rapids. At each stage of the short trip he asked me questions about which river we were on.

'How far down the Perene will we have to go,' he asked in perfect English, 'to reach the Ene? Twenty years ago, in 1962, I travelled from the Apurímac all the way down to the Ucayali river by raft. It took us four days.' He asked if the craft could go faster; on an open stretch of water I obliged.

But the schedule had to move on, and the President was starting to look at his watch. I returned to the bank and my passengers climbed out. The President insisted that the TV cameraman went for a ride to film the small rapids below the Mission. After a few explanations of the various parts of the craft, the visitors were taken to a room in the Mission, where a buffet lunch was laid out. Speeches and presentations had been planned. The President listened to a speech by the president of the local Campa village and replied, but then cut short the ceremony and made his way back to the Buffalo, well behind schedule after his enthusiastic interest in the River Rover.

As the Buffalo's engines were ready to start, Miguel's Cessna touched down unannounced, bearing Felix Perez, with Moises and Edmundo. The others hung back, disappointed that they had arrived too late to meet the President, but Miguel, true to character, strode up and shook Belaúnde by the hand as the President was about to get into the Buffalo.

75

The Cessna left for San Francisco almost as quickly as the Buffalo, but not before we had put Stu in its spare seat. It would lighten the hovercraft's load, and Stu could do some aerial filming of the valley on the way.

While Jim went off with Father Castillo to see if there was any petrol we could buy, I asked the nuns if they would like to ride in the craft. They rushed off to change into habits more suitable for hovercraft riding; the new outfits were topped by giant white sombreros. As their apprehension changed to delight at the new experience, I felt that we had made some recompense for their hospitality.

When the ten gallons of fuel arrived, I went in search of Father Castillo to pay for it. But he would take no money: neither for the petrol nor for our lodging.

'It is better to give than to receive,' he said, and was immovable on the subject. We left Puerto Ocopa, at midday exactly, touched by the warmth and generosity we had been shown, despite our unsought intrusion into their very special occasion.

Mike Cole sat back in the River Rover with a sigh. The important part was over; now we simply had to get back to San Francisco. But he could not relax for long.

'For better or for worse,' he said, his alert mind always ranging over every aspect of the team's activity, 'they will have tried the up-river push by now.'

I thought back over the events of the last few days. Before Julian's radio message, other plans had been made. Mike Duke and I were to take a craft up the river for no other purpose than to see how far we could get. We would just keep going. I had awaited the challenge with eager anticipation.

The tidy arrangement was not to be. We had already learned not to cling too closely to our plans in this project, but to accept changes of direction as a subtle hint from God. Mike Cole had decided that I should go with him to Puerto Ocopa. Mike Duke was then put in charge of the up-river trip. That was to prove another adventure in itself.

The team of four set off up the now swollen river. During the last four or five days torrential thunderstorms had washed

76

eroded soil and debris into the tributaries, changing the clear glacier water to a muddy brown.

There were dozens of rapids to climb. But every so often they came to a really bad one. The Indians call them *barrials*. Often the main thrust is *across* the general direction of the current; for where the river bends, its waters are funnelled violently against a rock barrier. The ricocheting flow then strikes huge rocks in mid-river and evolves a pattern of standing waves, in some cases metres high. On either side the turbulent water works itself into a milk-white frenzy, cascading past the sombre grey rocks which jut out menacingly from the bank.

In all, the team were to encounter five *barrials* on their trip up-river. Many vital decisions had to be taken on their journey, for an error of judgment could wreck the craft and endanger the mini-team. Mike often seemed to have Hobson's choice. The height of the waves could slow the hovercraft down until it reached parity with the current. Then Mike would have to leave the carefully chosen path. To go left might mean ending up on the rocks; to go right meant facing standing waves and gaping troughs. If wave peaks are farther apart than half the length of the craft, the air cushion dissipates. Losing its lift, the hovercraft falls into the water, and comes to a jarring standstill.

At the first *barrial* Mike decided to risk the waves. Leaving Allen Wells and Dick Bell on shore to keep the weight down, he took only Doug with him. He used his utmost skill, but half-way up the hovercraft ran out of momentum: it would not budge. He resigned himself to retreating back down the rapid. That too needed skill. He reduced power carefully, and the River Rover started to fall backwards, then skidded sideways down the length of the *barrial*.

How could this obstacle be surmounted? While the four men did not want to turn back, the hovercraft was a precious asset and not lightly to be hazarded. There was one possibility – to skirt the giant waves as tightly as possible; make a sharp turn to the left across smooth water; then up the left-hand edge of the rapid, keeping close to the huge boulders. The speed had to be exactly right, and the turn executed at the precise spot. Mike doubted his own skill, but River Rover's unique controls were designed for this sort of work. Mike did not believe in luck.

77

Experience had taught him that God was sovereign. He offered his skills to God, and asked Him, of His supernatural power, to give direction, prompting and safety.

'We'll give it a go,' he said simply. 'Come on, Doug.' Allen sat on the biggest boulder to give a point of aim. Dick moved further up-river to position himself for photography – and to pray.

At their second run, Mike did not hear the shouts of encouragement, nor see the fists punching the air, willing River Rover to reach the top. He was totally absorbed in his task. A cloud of spray showed that this time his efforts had been successful. Leaping in the air in his excitement, Dick let out a resounding 'Alleluia' – and landed in the water next to the rock on which he had been standing.

'Wasn't it terrific?'

'Did you see her go?'

'That was close, wasn't it?'

'Praise God!'

Dick and Allen's elation was short-lived. In the heat Allen had stripped to bathing costume and boots. Dick, carrying his camera, was fully clothed and working his way up-river through reeds growing at the water's edge. Suddenly, he felt something sharp sting his arm. 'That's a nasty thorn bush,' he exclaimed, then saw with horror that his arm was covered with wasps. Unwittingly, he had disturbed their nest!

'Wasps! Run!' he yelled to Allen – and set off through the reeds like an Olympic sprinter, taking only a few wasps with him.

Allen went headlong into the mêlée of buzzing, distressed, revenge-seeking insects. The swarm enveloped and attacked him with ferocity. Wasps were in his hair, and were stinging every part of his body. Allen yelled and dived into the river, staying under the oozing, muddy water for as long as his lungs could stand the strain. The wasps drowned; but by now their venom was circulating in Allen's bloodstream.

Gingerly he clambered out and followed Dick's trail as easily as if it had been an elephant's. Bruised, very sore, and feeling strange from the poison's effect on his nervous system, he made it to the hovercraft. It took ten minutes to apply antiseptic cream to each of the fifty angry lumps distributed over his body. The wasps must have been only moderately venomous. Had it not been so, Allen would never have made it back to England. He silently thanked the medical team for their painstaking preparation of personal medical kits, and the Piriton tablets he'd been able to take to counteract the allergic reaction and reduce the swelling.

The four adventurers clambered into the hovercraft. It had taken exactly an hour to conquer this *barrial*. The journey to San Martín took up the next forty-five minutes.

At San Martín James McClune, Paul Turton and Brian Holdsworth were busy constructing the tank which was to bring a clean water supply to the village. The mini-team filled up the hovercraft tanks, and off-loaded as much weight as could be spared in kit and fuel. The hovercraft was ready to leave for the next stage of the journey. Simultaneously, the medical team arrived by canoe from up-river. Having just passed through the next *barrial* to be faced by the hovercraft team, and rough water further up-river, they were doubtful that River Rover would make it. Horace and David, the two doctors, undertook to pray for the four throughout the rest of the day.

Twenty minutes after departure, 05 met the next *barrial*, the first hovercraft ever to do so. Across the whole width of the river, the water hammered down mercilessly, and burst up with explosive ferocity as it hit hidden boulders. The group's first reaction was 'Let's give it a miss.' They stood on the bank, disconsolate, and were joined by a Peruvian farmer, who punted across the river on his balsa raft. He shook his head.

'Very dangerous!'

They knew that.

'No way up this side!'

They agreed.

'No way up at all!'

They disagreed. They had not fully examined the *barrial* for themselves.

Mike Duke is meticulous and practical. He flew as a British Airways flight engineer for a number of years and now teaches other engineers in the company's school. Taking Doug with him, he made a careful, and prayerful, analysis of the problem. There was one possibility, a narrow gap between a rock on the right, and a trough to the left. It would be a 'one-off' opportunity, with no room for error. If Mike failed to get through first time there would be no second attempt.

River Rover 05 had been taken across the river and tied to a tree and some rocks. Mike and Doug returned to it after their hour-long assessment to find Allen and Dick at the ropes, pulling hard against the strong current, in an endeavour to prevent 05 from uprooting the tree to which she was tied.

'Well?' Dick asked. 'Are you going to give it a go?'

Delay would jeopardise any further adventure ahead. It was now two thirty p.m. With Dick's persuasion and promise of supporting prayers, Mike agreed to try. He was clearly unhappy. But he was also resolved.

Mike followed his planned route, concentrating on the almost superhuman task. The craft started to skid; there was a deafening crack and 05 collided with the rock. From inside the cabin it sounded as if the whole machine had disintegrated. Then, with Mike's instant and correct handling, the craft responded and flew up the rest of the rapid.

Allen and Dick rushed up as Mike landed on a narrow sand-bank. 'Well done!' they exclaimed. 'Brilliant. That was terrific!'

Mike was dubious. 'We really thumped her on that rock,' he said unhappily. 'I hate to think what damage I did.'

'From outside, it didn't sound at all bad,' Allen replied.

All four got down in the sand to inspect the hull. To their amazement, they could find nothing wrong.

'Thank you, Father,' whispered Dick.

Making time for a drink and a bite of chocolate, they pressed on. Mike Duke asked Doug to drive. Doug had been on the expedition to Nepal in 1979, and had driven the Mark 2 on the Kali Gandaki river. But this was Mark 3, with different controls. Dick, knowing the treacherous river between San Martín and Lechemayo, questioned the wisdom of allowing Doug to drive. But Mike, sitting next to Doug, was confident. And his decision, as Captain, was final.

Doug found himself in rougher waters than he had ever

The four doctors from Brixham

Mothers and babies given priority

From Falklands to Amazon dentist — Andy Prosser

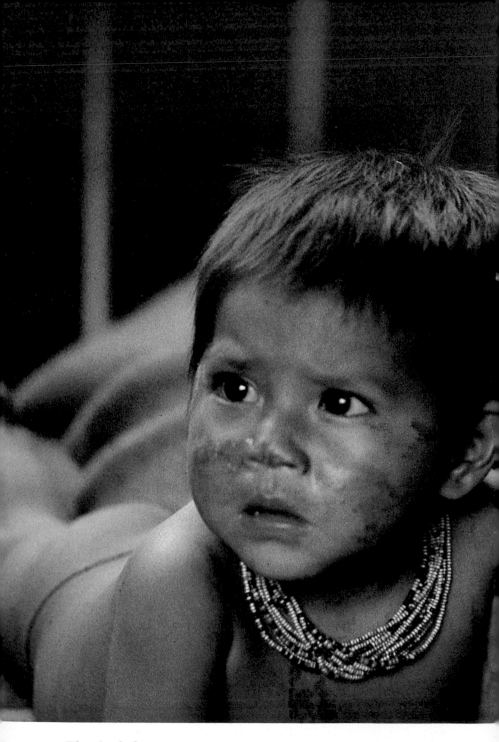

Plea for help

Mike Cole about to enjoy Campa hospitality

driven through before. But, with Mike's prompting, he pressed on and found a way through. His concentration was so intense that he did not notice when they reached Lechemayo. The other three shouted at him to stop, and the bearded mariner returned them to dry land.

They climbed up the rugged pathway to the familiar shop. People came down to look at the hovercraft, there for the first time. The four relaxed with a Coke, as Dick chatted to the shopkeeper. On the very first clinic visit, so many weeks before, he had brought his son on a wheelbarrow to have his festering sore cleaned and cured.

'How is your son?' Dick asked.

'*Muy bueno,*' the man replied. 'Fine.' He pointed outside to where the boy was running around, enjoying himself.

'And your wife?' Dick asked. His wife was the person, on that same first clinic, for whom there was no medicine. She had been shivering with malaria, and Dick had felt prompted to go to her and pray for her recovery.

'*Bueno.* She is fine,' the shopkeeper replied.

'The malaria?' Dick asked. She had not returned to subsequent clinics, so we had no news of her condition.

'Oh, that. She was cured straight away after you had prayed for her.'

Dick joyfully asked that the woman be brought in, and prayed again for the couple and their family, his arms around them both. He prayed that God might move supernaturally in them, strengthen their faith and heal their bodies.

In his gratitude the shopkeeper gave the four *gringos* a pineapple as they climbed back into the River Rover. The *barrial* just round the corner was the acid test in their up-river push. None of the team had gone beyond this point.

Carefully choosing his path, Mike Duke selected full power and headed for the third *barrial*. The craft stopped twice during the run, but Mike skilfully got her going again. As if sneering at the anti-climax, 05 was soon gracefully emerging from the top of the rapid.

The river narrowed, and the hills inched their way inward, until they were no longer background, but formed the edge of the river. The valley became a gorge. Still they pressed on, shrugging off minor setbacks in the turbulent water and surviving the towering waves of the fourth *barrial*.

The fifth *barrial* was quieter than it would normally have been, because of the increase in water content. Mike picked his way carefully amongst the boulders, turning and twisting the responsive craft. Beyond it, a welcome stretch of sand appeared on the left. Mike drove gently up it and switched off. It was four p.m.

Mike turned to the others.

'I'm not sure how long it will take to get back to San Martín, and we have to be there by five thirty at the latest. I guess we have to stop here. Besides that, we haven't got enough petrol to get much further.' They reluctantly agreed. Tired, but still keen to go further, they allowed common sense to prevail. Mike inscribed 'JS EXPEDITION 1982' on a stone and took a photograph of it. Future generations of Peruvians will perhaps wonder what it means.

A local man and his two daughters fought their way through the undergrowth to see the visitors. They asked him where they were.

'Quaperos,' he replied. They were none the wiser, but at least they could report that they had reached it! It was about 16 kilometres above Lechemayo, which was the normal head of canoe travel.

River Rover went down rapids more controllably in a side slip than straight on, and it took them fifty-three minutes to get down to San Martín, and a further six minutes to find a safe parking place. At five twenty-five they walked up the path to the village, past the football pitch, and along past the school to the clinic. They were just in time to enjoy an appetising candle-light meal prepared by the medical team.

It had been a good day. They had fought the Great Speaker – and won. God had given them success, as they had asked.

The up-river party made their way back to San Francisco on Saturday morning. By that afternoon Mike Cole, Jim Mudie and I were returning too, bringing 06 back from Puerto Ocopa. Although we knew nothing of their triumph, we were flushed with our own success.

Rounding the last of many bends, climbing the last of many rapids, we arrived at base camp in time for the short Sunday morning service. I quietly thanked God for the safe completion of a journey which had never been part of our plan, but assuredly was part of His.

CHAPTER SEVEN

Swords into Scalpels

AN OLD MAN walked slowly into the jungle health post, his awkward gait showing his pain. The skin on his wrinkled face was gnarled and toughened like old leather. His eyes were tired and glazed, as if he were living in a different world.

'*Cual es su problema, viejo,*' asked Dick Bell kindly. 'What is your problem, old man?'

The old man's answer was laboriously translated from Quechua into Spanish, and then into English as Bill Gould listened patiently.

'My legs, they are swollen.'

Bill examined the sinewy limbs, and set him on a course of penicillin for the infection, telling him to return next week.

'*Gracias. Muchas gracias.*' The man was very grateful. He exchanged a few measly *soles* for the medicine, but then hesitated. Obviously there was something else bothering him.

'What is it, old man?' Dick asked.

Slowly and reluctantly, as if already knowing the answer, he asked, 'Is it all right if I drink *cerveza*, beer?'

'No.' Bill's reply was short and definite.

'Cigarettes?' asked the old man. Bill hesitated. Reluctantly he said, 'Yes, if you must.'

The man paused. 'Can I continue to chew coca?'

'No! Definitely not!' Bill was adamant. 'No coca.' It became very obvious that the dear old fellow's far-away look resulted as much from his coca-chewing habit as from his pain or senility. Indeed, the coca leaves, the raw material of the process that results in cocaine, would be helping to deaden his pain. The

84

old man was crestfallen, but Bill was adamant. The harm done by the coca far outweighed the anaesthetic effects. The vicious circle had to be broken somewhere.

The incident was short-lived. The old man hobbled away, and we never knew how long he followed the 'doctor's orders', if at all.

It had been almost impossible, before arriving in San Francisco, to make detailed plans and schedules for the medical expedition. Any that we did make were swept away in the waves of changing circumstances. As soon as we arrived, though, when the hovercraft engineering and training work had got under way, Mike Cole was eager to get the powerful medical team to work.

Since Ross Adley, who had done much of the preparation work, could not be with us in Peru, it was Bill Gould who explained to the rest of us what the team of medical and dental experts intended.

'Our major purpose,' he said as we sat at our trestle tables after a filling Base Camp meal, 'is training.'

'Although we will be using vastly superior resources for the short time we are here, we will always have to bear in mind the facilities that will exist after we have gone. The *sanitario*, the village health worker, will gain nothing at all if we just treat patients and then move on. Every case is an opportunity to train the *sanitario* in some particular aspect of medicine.'

The medics planned to visit each of the ten health posts once a week. There had been a discussion about the frequency of the clinics, since some of the team felt that a fortnightly clinic would be quite sufficient for the size of the villages involved.

'That may be true,' commented Bill, applying a little Third World psychology, 'but these people are much more likely to turn up if they know we will come on a particular day of the week at a given time. If they have to worry about which weeks we will come, they just won't bother.'

Cathy agreed. 'And if you don't appear on the appointed day, they will quickly give up. We have to tell them when we are coming, and then make absolutely sure that we are reliable and punctual.'

85

In discussion with Julian, the medics had worked out a punishing weekly schedule. For the time being, the group would have to make its river journeys in Mario's canoe, which was expensive to run, but the size of the medical team justified the larger load capacity.

The schedule was split into two separate 'trips', one up and the other down the water highway. The down-river run lasted two days, after which the weary travellers would stumble into camp, often laden with gifts of pineapples, oranges, avocadoes or bananas, just before dusk to share their news. They would thankfully retire into their own tents for a good night's sleep, but the next day they would be on the move again, this time for three days.

Sunday was a rest day, but on Monday they would be working again, this time a little closer to home. About forty-five minutes' walk up the hill behind our camp was a small Campa Indian village; the medical team would walk up there on Monday morning to hold a two-hour clinic, and walk back in time for a meal at midday. Monday afternoon was for 'catching up' – re-stocking with medications from the pharmacy they had established in the operations centre, planning the coming week, and dealing with any medical problems on the team.

The routine was wearing, and often seemed little different from their work at home, but there was a variety in the style and character of the villages, which lightened the burden.

While most of our work was with the stoical and colourful Quechua Indians, the direct descendants of the Incas, two of the clinics were in Campa villages, Otari and Sampantuari. This totally separate ethnic group shows little concession to the twentieth century, and lives in a tight tribal system with an all-powerful chief. The silent enigmatic hunters, their haunted faces straight out of the Stone Age, dress in long, loose cinnamon-coloured cotton robes, or *cushmas*; they are true jungle Indians. Many groups have melted into the vastness of Amazonia at the advance of the Quechua settlers, but some have firmly stood their ground.

Although the Campas maintained their very separate lifestyle and language, many now spoke Spanish, and the groups kept up a wary contact with the outside world. Normally one of their number would be chosen by the chief to be their 'contact man' for a period of two or three years, before melting back into the tribe. The clinic at Otari was shared with Quechua farmers who lived nearby; eventually, each community would provide a *sanitario*.

Of the ten health posts, the best, without doubt, was Sivia. The spotlessly clean *puesto de salud* was surrounded by neat, well-kept flower beds, and its quiet serenity was always a welcome contrast to the town's brash, bustling market by the riverside. The post was run by two marvellous Spanish nuns; it had a small pharmacy and two separate treatment rooms, and the sisters helped the middle-aged *sanitario* with a calm and dedicated efficiency. The patients were mostly Quechua merchants and farmers and their children; despite the relative prosperity of the town, malnutrition as a result of intestinal worms was the predominant problem. But the easy availability of medical help often led to the attitudes of the 'civilized' world – many patients complained of simply feeling tired or vaguely unwell.

Few of the other clinics approached the standard of Sivia's. Although most had a completed health post building there were a few where the *puesto* was little more than an empty shell. Where this was the case, as in Canaire or Boca del Mantaro, the medical team had no *sanitario* to deal with or train, and they would make all of their arrangements with the village hierarchy. In most Quechua villages, the power was held by the *teniente*, who was usually a relatively young man; in contrast to British local politics, it is the young – those with the energy to get things done – who hold the responsibility.

When there was a *sanitario*, the health work could go on for the whole time, not just during the weekly visit. It was important that the *sanitario* did not save all his or her patients until the *gringos* arrived, and that the patients in turn did not lose faith in their *sanitario*.

The most distant up-river health post was at Lechemayo, where the inward-facing houses were built around a square of turf, whose centrepiece was a standpipe supplying relatively clean water. The clinic, a substantial blue concrete building standing in a fenced enclosure at the edge of the village, had a roof, and mosquito nets on most of the windows, quite a luxury by local standards.

The first visit to each village had been planned as a fact-finding session, and the team had prepared a questionnaire to establish the basic facts. At Lechemayo, they knew, there was a *sanitario* by the name of Marcos, but he was away in Ayacucho doing a course in laboratory work. The doctors asked for the chief to come, and started to fill in the questionnaire.

'How many people in the village? How old is the oldest person?' (the answer to this second question was invariably 120).

'How many children go to school?'

'There are 100 in the school here.'

'How many teachers?'

'Two.'

'What are the ages of the children in school?'

'They go to school at the age of five. They have to remain there until they are thirteen or fourteen, but some are still there at sixteen.'

'How many of the adults can read and write?'

'About half. You see,' the chief added confidentially, 'most of them have come down from the Andes, and in the mountains there are no schools.'

'Have the children been given their pre-school inoculations?'

The answer to that had to be spelled out in detail. They had all had their polio, T.A.B.T., cholera, smallpox and yellow fever immunisation. The doctors were impressed.

'We had much illness here three years ago. It was yellow fever, and many of our people died. There was great distress in the mountains, and whole villages died before we knew about it.'

'What happened?' asked the visitors, fascinated.

'Don Julian. He sent up the medicine. He came with some others. They took Marcos and they went everywhere they could and gave this medicine to everyone they found. We got the message out to all who could hear, and they came for many days to our village, where they had their injection. Now,' the chief said smiling, 'there is no yellow fever, and the people are well.'

88

Marcos had since been around the village with every vaccination except tetanus and rabies. It seemed as if he had no serum
for those. We hardly expected such medical sophistication so
far from civilisation.

The team had planned only to learn on this visit, and not to
treat. Needless to say, when presented with scores of beseeching
faces, their intention weakened and they ended up providing
treatment, and gaining their first insight into the scale of
the need. A small child with rickets so obvious that even the
dentists could recognise it, arrived not as a patient, but pushing
a wheelbarrow containing a far more seriously ill baby, who
was later diagnosed as having typhoid.

The pattern continued. Directly opposite Lechemayo on
the opposite bank was Villa Virgen, the village which had just
welcomed back its *sanitaria*, Rebecca, during our visit in 1981.
Since then, half of the village had been destroyed. A huge scar
marked the hillside on the opposite bank where thousands of
tons of earth had slipped into and across the river engulfing
the huts, taking over thirty lives and damming the river into a
four-kilometre lake for several hours.

The medical visitors got to know Rebecca. She was an
attractive dimple-cheeked girl with long dark curly hair,
who had brought a feminine feel for design to the *puesto de
salud*, with flowers on the table and colourful posters on the
wall.

It was obvious that those who were left in Villa Virgen were
facing the future cheerfully and courageously. 'Perhaps,' said
Dick Bell, 'it's because eighty per cent of the villagers attend
the evangelical chapel.'

The up- and down-river trips were not confined to medical
experts. The departures on Tuesday and Thursday mornings
were a major event at Base Camp. At seven a.m. (or eight, or
nine, or whatever time the canoe, the engines, the fuel and the
boatman could be assembled in one place at one time) they
would leave. The boat always looked full: two doctors, two
dentists, one or two nurses, an 'administrator', an interpreter
and whoever else had a job to do at one of the villages. The
administrator, normally Chris or Tim or Brian, was there to
take charge of the cooking and setting up beds, etc. In the long

term, the Peruvian doctors would have beds permanently set up, but for us that was not feasible.

Interpretation was more of a problem. A Spanish-speaker from the team would always be at each clinic. Sometimes it was Paul Turton or 'Ricardo' Ball, when Roy could spare them from the workshop. For several weeks it was Dick Bell; his grammar was not perfect, but he made up for it by his enthusiasm and compassionate concern. There were several of the patients for whom he believed he should pray for healing; the reaction of the medical team was mixed – some felt frustrated that he was a barrier between them and their patients, others felt that prayer was an entirely appropriate reaction to the horrific squalor and disease we were witnessing.

Two visitors we had not planned to use as interpreters were photographer Tony Prime and journalist Ian Mather of the *Observer*. Released on bail after three months in an Argentinian gaol, they had bravely returned to South America to visit us. Their Spanish was adequate, but clearly betrayed the unusual circumstances in which they had learned it.

Villagers learned that we meant it when we said 'Come back next week.' But the standard of health was inconsistent through the valley; it depended on the interest and enthusiasm of the local people. One clinic, San Martín, had not had a *sanitario* appointed.

'They only have a *sanitario*,' said Julian firmly, 'if they have finished their health post.' San Martín's health post was in a poor state, and the people showed no urgency to complete it.

One evening as the team sat over their meal at San Martín, an unfamiliar villager collared Dick Bell and started to talk at length about his brother. This brother was medically trained, had lots of qualifications, and could we recommend him as *sanitario* at San Martín? Dick only barely got the gist of what the man wanted. In the end, he was able to say that it was not up to us to select or recommend anyone for the post. It was Don Julian's task. Go and see him. Anyway, why wasn't the brother there himself to offer? We later discovered that both this man and his brother were Maoists, and wanted the position as a base for their terrorist activities.

90

The same evening, two local boys arrived and tried to persuade the doctors to walk with them to a settlement some ten kilometres away where, they said, twenty to thirty people were in an advanced state of T.B. At this point the medics were unable to do anything without depriving another clinic of their time, but promised to do what they could on a subsequent visit. Yet, as they stared into the fire, each of them wondered how empty those words really were. The problem of treating tuberculosis is two-fold. Firstly, the combination drugs are very expensive and we had all too few at our disposal, and secondly, Third-World peoples do not understand the necessity for continuing treatment after the symptoms have cleared up. In the case of T.B., this is for several months. One drug that we had brought with us, though, was simple and effective, and the doctors arranged for long-term treatment to be made available through the Amazon Trust.

David Langley later diagnosed pulmonary T.B. in a man of thirty. He started him on isozone forte for a year, giving him a month's supply straight away, and asked after his family.

'My mother is bad,' he said.

'With what?'

'Just like me. She spits blood and coughs a lot.' She was outside, so David invited her in. Sure enough, she had T.B. too. David gave her the same medicine.

'And do you have any more family?' he asked, getting suspicious.

'Si, señor. I have three children, aged fifteen, nine, and six.'

'Are they bad too?'

'I'm afraid so, señor. They also keep us awake at night with their coughs.'

We told them to bring the children back the following week, which he did. Sure enough, they all had it. T.B. is contagious.

Our language problem at the clinics was a double difficulty. Even though we had expertise in Spanish available, many of the patients spoke only Quechua. The problem was eased when Julian appointed a Peruvian nurse who would continue the work after we had left. Ene spoke good Quechua and Spanish and was therefore able to delve more deeply into the patients' problems. At times, though, in her brusque, efficient way, she would 'take over' the patient and cut out the doctors who were meant to be instructing her. Her main complaint with the doctors was their annoying habit of refusing to give a patient medicine if he did not need it; to her mind, if someone had taken the trouble to come, they deserved to take something away with them.

Our own nurse, Louise Arrow, had been reducing the load on the doctors, day after day, long before Ene arrived, and she continued to work in the clinics alongside the Peruvian nurse. Louise's quiet and soft femininity was deceptive; for it hid a powerful and determined Christianity. Before taking up nursing, she had been an international-class show jumper, until an accident had threatened to cripple her for life. Sheer guts had enabled her to walk again.

Of the medical team, only the dentists went out on every trip and served every clinic. Fiery, forthright Cathy and calm, self-contained Andy went on pulling teeth, instructing the *sanitarios*, and teaching the children about preventive dentistry, day in, day out for the full eight weeks. Admittedly, the occasional tooth was extracted by an eager engineer, but by the end of the expedition the pair had taken out over 500 teeth.

The doctors, of course, changed over half-way through our time. Former medical missionary Bill Gould and former Gurkha M.O. David Wood handed over to a pair who, in contrast, had no experience of tropical medicine. However, the ground had been well prepared, and David Langley and Horace Pile slipped smoothly into the schedule of weekly clinics.

On one jungle walk, the two doctors became separated from their companions and took a short cut, David leading confidently and Horace trotting obediently behind. After half an hour, they became totally, hopelessly lost in the hostile jungle. They stopped where they were and prayed, casting their safety on to God. Shortly afterwards, they met a small boy, who pointed vaguely with his arm; following his directions, they almost immediately came upon the only path that was familiar to them. Any passing *campesino* would have been amazed to see two *gringo* doctors leaping and dancing about, shouting 'Praise the Lord' at the tops of their voices.

David, on his first clinic visit, was amazed by the common-place nature of complaints which would be rarities at home: anaemia caused by hookworm, nephritis, or a five-year-old hip fracture which had been completely untreated, resulting in four inches of thigh muscle wasting away. With his analytical approach, he carefully documented the reasons for the con-tinuing failure of fifty per cent of babies in one village to reach their first birthday: gastro-enteritis; respiratory infections; and neo-natal septicaemia/tetanus caused by cutting the umbilical cord with a rusty razor-blade. What chance does a child have?

Horace, on the other hand, was particularly taken with the gentle Campa people. The Campa clinics were held in airy palm-thatch huts, with the whole village looking on. At the team's first visit to Otari, chief Amadeo, his face daubed with red paint, had launched into a hostile diatribe about the Peruvian Government, the Amazon Trust and perfidious white people generally. He was most nonplussed when the team politely let him finish and then stepped forward to shake his hand; they had understood not a word! Amadeo's manner softened, especially when he learned that our engineers might be able to fix his ancient outboard motor. The following week he presented himself for dental treatment.

Amadeo loved to receive gifts from visitors, and set his beady eyes on Andy Prosser's pen. Could he have it?

'Of course he can,' said Mike Cole, and Andy lost the first of many vanishing items of equipment, with his usual unruffled equanimity. To Andy, the expedition was easy compared with his Falklands experience with the Royal Marines. He was always immaculately turned out, always clean-shaven. The Colonel had insisted that they shaved in the biting South Atlantic winds; to do so in the jungle was no hardship.

Unlike the Quechua *tenientes*, elected as village organisers, the Campa chiefs were autocratic rulers. For example, the chief ran the economy of the village. All finance passed through him, and he provided for his people. If any of them earned money outside, they gave it all to the chief, who redistributed it throughout the community as was fair. Thus he detailed some to buy food, and where to buy it, giving them the money. He decided who was to hunt, what they were to hunt, and where

93

they were to hunt. He decided what crops were to be planted and where, and who was to do it. When a chief said to his people that they should have nothing to do with the tribe next door, then that was what had to happen.

The inter-tribal squabbles of the Campas affected the pro-vision we could make for their health. One evening, I had a long conversation with two Campas, from a village we did not know, as they set off for a night hunting trip.

'Can't you do a clinic for us as well as Sampantuari?' pleaded one of them, in Spanish. The group lived very close to our Monday clinic, numbered about forty, and they had cases of T.B. and anaemia.

'We can't,' I said, 'you must go to Sampantuari.'

The 'representative' was intelligent and sophisticated, despite his Stone Age bow and arrows – he had studied at college in Pucallpa. A cheap digital watch clashed with his ochre-toned *cushma*.

'My people are afraid,' he said. 'They think that the Sampantuari people will kill them if they go there. Our villages have been fighting for many years.'

The conversation continued. I tried to persuade him that *now* was the time to establish their right to share the clinic, while we were still there. The black-haired hunter smiled sadly, and agreed to try and persuade his chief to come to the clinic. So far as we knew, they never came.

At one of the clinics there was an eighty-year-old Campa woman, who looked thirty. She had smooth skin, of which many a Western lady would be envious, black hair and a full set of smiling teeth. Horace asked some leading questions.

'How many are there in your family?'

'I have three children, four grandchildren, and two great grandchildren,' she said sweetly.

'How do you manage to look so young?' the amazed Horace asked.

'I chewed a leaf when I was younger as a contraceptive. Then I chewed another leaf as a fertility drug so that I could have my family when I wanted to. And I chew another leaf to keep my teeth clean,' she grinned, delighted with our pleasure in her youthful looks.

We checked up on it later. The U.K. contraceptive pill was first produced from a plant found only in the forests of Amazonia. We asked her for a sample, but she could not or would not give us one. We asked a pharmacist in San Francisco about the fertility drug, and she was unable to verify or deny its existence. As for the teeth, the dentists said that chewing anything kept the saliva glands working, which operated as a cleansing agent for the teeth. Nevertheless, this old girl had obviously discovered – or had had handed down – some useful herbal hints.

It was a hike of about forty-five minutes to reach the clinic at the little Quechua village of Palma Pampa. The shady path led between fields of innocuous-looking verdant coca bushes. Each *campesino*, or farmer, was allowed to grow up to two acres of the crop 'for his own use'; the leaves are chewed to relieve pain or hunger, or infused to make a tea which is said to be good for altitude sickness. Yet the leaves are also processed into pure cocaine, which enslaves thousands on the inner city streets of the Western world. Though coca-growing is legal, there is an automatic fifteen-year sentence for the production of *pasta básica* or cocaine paste, the essential interim stage of the process. Nevertheless, the drug traffickers thrive on their smuggling activities; the $300 they pay the farmer, for a two-acre crop, represents a street value of perhaps $12 million in New York or Chicago. Ironically, at that price, the poor *campesino* cannot afford not to grow the debilitating crop; coffee or cocoa would earn him much less. The little town of San Francisco is full of flashy cars and ostentatious consumer goods financed on the back of the illegal trade. The sums of money involved are so huge that murder, corruption and extortion are inevitable results.

Although Julian's medical and other work to improve the well-being of the people is indirectly part of the fight against the cocaine trade, we were hypercautious about any involvement with the *narcotraficantes* or drug traffickers. Nevertheless, through a curious connection, they held up our hovercraft operations for several days. All of the Lucas batteries we had brought were dry-charged – they needed sulphuric acid. But sulphuric acid is essential to the cocaine process, and is a controlled substance in the *selva*. Even when we obtained a special permit to buy acid, the only quantities for sale were at extortionate prices adjusted to the illegal market. We sent for acid from Ayacucho by road, preferring to wait rather than pay the inflated price.

We had with us 26 twelve-volt batteries; they were not all for the hovercraft. All of the high-frequency radio sets we had bought from A.E.L. for the health posts were battery-driven. During the latter part of our time in the Apurímac, having completed the hovercraft radio installations, Doug Cooledge started to move out to the health posts. He travelled with the medical team on their regular journeys, being dropped off here or there with a helper to aid him in finding and erecting a suitable pole for the aerial. Not every *puesto* had a *sanitario*, so some of our radios had to stay in the store for safety's sake.

One by one, tall masts, hacked from the jungle, would sprout next to the little blue health posts, and Doug's gruff tones would come through loud and clear at San Francisco, as he showed the fascinated *sanitarios* how they could speak to the operations centre. The battery-driven sets were an essential link in the medical chain.

During the initial health questionnaire, the villagers had been asked one very important question: 'What is your greatest need?'

At almost every village, the answer had been 'Clean water.' Welsh Water Authority engineer John Riden began systematically to survey the villages for a simple, safe water supply.

He had very little time available with us, but John was determined to do the job he had come for. Mike disagreed and changed John's terms of reference. He felt that we needed to make a concrete contribution somewhere – actually to give a village clean water. Reports are fine, but they can gather dust for a decade. Clean water could save lives right away.

'But,' said John in his lilting Welsh voice, 'then I won't finish the surveys.' The discussion became heated, but eventually a compromise was reached, as Mike brought James McClune's contribution into the calculation.

'I'll be helping with the work,' said the willing James. 'I'm sure that we can achieve something.' As the weeks went by, the two combined the survey with a major clean water project at the village of San Martín. They selected a stream which seemed to have no contamination further up, tapped the water off and led it by narrow pipes to a tap in the village, with a concrete tank in the line to allow sediment to drop out. Julian supplied the cement, the team supplied the expertise and the willing villagers and school children supplied the manpower.

After John had returned to the Welsh hills, Paul Turton lent a hand, and later Brian Holdsworth took over the work of building the concrete tank. By the time we left, the simple clean water system was operational, a boon to San Martín, and a working example for the other villages to follow. We helped financially with a similar water supply for the little evangelical Christian community up the hill from San Francisco. The dedication service was a blend of deep reverence and easy hilarity; after the pastor's word about Jesus being the water of life, James was persuaded to wash his shock of unruly hair under the makeshift shower.

Clean water in the villages had been one of our expedition goals. Each of these projects finished with a time of dedication and thanksgiving. Because the villagers had been involved in the work, their delight was as great as our own.

The emphasis throughout our medical work was on prevention rather than cure: clean drinking water and not expensive medicines; hygienic latrines rather than treatment for dysentery. The medics quickly established a 'Top Twenty' list of basic medicines to equip the health posts. Anything more was an over-complication, and represented unnecessary expense. The Amazon Trust had persuaded us to make a consultation charge of 500 *soles*, and to charge the same for each drug. Reluctantly, we agreed – in the long term, the clinics would have to make a small charge – but the Campas were charged nothing. If anyone could not pay, we did not insist.

The principles of clean water and simple hygiene would go a long way towards bringing health to these sturdy people. We knew how easy it was for disease to spread in our squalid tropical surroundings. Despite our attempts to maintain our isolation, Tony Maher was pole-axed by typhoid and was confined to his camp bed for many days.

Tony recovered sufficiently, though, to play a minor role

in the final act of the medical team – the symposium. The fine-sounding name described a two-day training session for all of the valley's *sanitarios* and schoolteachers to consolidate the eight weeks of teaching. Cathy, Andy, Louise, David and Horace taught the use of the 'Top Twenty', the safe preparation of food and water, the construction of latrines, first aid, health care for the under-fives and their mothers, and many other related topics. And Tony's role? With a gory broken leg, he was the 'victim' of a fall from a tall tree – but only for first aid demonstration purposes!

In our last week at San Francisco, after Dick Bell had taken the training process as far as he could, we took the next logical step. The confident Moises was sent off down river in the hovercraft, with Ene the nurse and Dr. David Langley aboard, and with Ricardo Ball as engineer and interpreter. The four completed the two-day down-river clinic run without major occurrence; although there was still much to learn, and much support would be needed, we could now confidently leave the River Rovers with their new Peruvian operators.

CHAPTER EIGHT

On the Move

W HEN MIKE COLE has mastered all the implications of an issue, he drives towards his goal with unrelenting persistence, brushing aside obstacles that would deter him from his primary aim. Right from the beginning he was set to take River Rover 06 down-river to the Christian group at Pucallpa, and not for anything was it going any other way. Besides, it was to be our main adventure – driving an untried craft on an uncharted river over an unknown number of days. No difficulty was going to get in our way. But difficulties there were.

Logistics was the first one. How much equipment could we take down? Where would we buy petrol? How many craft would we take?

Clearly, the hovercraft would never get there on its own. Most of the fuelling stops down-river would only cater for the outboard motors; the fuel would be two-stroke mix, and not *gasolina pura*. So we had to take fuel of our own. In any case, the team had been looking forward to this journey as the most challenging part of the expedition. How could Mike exclude anyone? All this meant taking a canoe and the two Gemini inflatables.

We needed more fuel. There was a tanker lorry to be sent for from the coast; an acceptable price to be negotiated; the laborious unloading of 45-gallon drums. It all took time.

Meanwhile a canoe had to be found. Mario was unhappy to let his boat go down to Pucallpa, as he could get a reasonable income from it plying up and down the Apurímac. Eventually he agreed – at a price. We were sorry to see Mario, one of

Julian's boys, treating the matter as a purely commercial pro-
position, with an eye on the *gringo*'s bottomless pockets. We
had hoped that the sacrifices that we all had made towards
bringing technology and help to the Apurímac would rub off.
Perhaps our thinking was too naive. Men are like that, and only
God can change them.

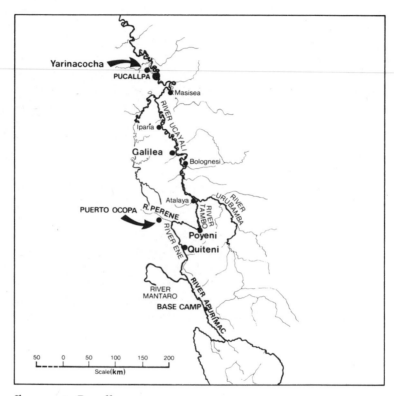

Journey to Pucallpa

We decided to take our Christian Base Camp worker, Maxi,
with us. Trustworthy, capable and unbelievably willing, Maxi
would be a real asset to our adventure. He had been negotiating
with Mario, his brother-in-law, for us, and we also asked him
to find us a boatman, as none of Julian's boys could come with

us. He unearthed a man called Horacio, who was to be both a thorn and a rose to us.

As our medical team were sorting out their medicines a difficulty emerged. We had brought with us crates and crates of medicines. Our experience on the job, though, had changed our opinion of what medicines were actually needed in the valley. So the doctors were rustling through bottles and bandages for four or five days, leaving everything that was necessary, and stock-piling everything that was not. Many U.K. firms had donated every kind of medicine for the expedition, and most of them were specialised medication, fit only for hospital use. These we decided to donate to a hospital in Lima that was sacrificially working among the poor. In the hands of non-specialised para-medics, some of the medicines could be dangerous.

There the problem began. Dr. Felix Perez, retired doctor and now administrator for the Amazon Trust in Lima, was horrified to see all those expensive medicines go.

His argument was simple. In the period of time that the expedition was delayed by the Falklands conflict, a certain lady lawyer in Lima had expressed doubts about the motives of the expedition. Dark innuendos about drug smuggling and grasping were raised; that was the 'bash the Brits' time in Peru. A decree was issued that *all* the equipment brought by the expedition to Peru legally belonged to the Amazon Trust, and was under their care and responsibility. All, that is, except Service equipment we had brought to do our job. So far, so good. At least the Amazon Trust could now clear it all from Customs, and transfer it to the Rio Apurímac. But legally, it meant that we could not do what we liked with what we had brought. The doctor stood his legal ground. The spirit of generosity which had governed all our actions and motives was now blasted to pieces.

Threats of resignation and legal battles flew about. Julian was devastated. He knew the legal position. He knew our motivation. The strain of being the man in the middle brought this extraordinary man to tears; it was the first and last time that we saw him so distraught. He knew that if he were to stand his ground with us, it could mean trouble for the Amazon Trust in Peru.

The medics were disheartened that a week's hard slog of

101

sorting out the medicines was totally wasted. The engineers reacted angrily, and tightened their belts. Their flexibility about leaving extra equipment at San Francisco suddenly melted away. Some decided that the well-known aphorism was differently understood here; here it was 'Always kick a gift horse in the teeth.'

Meanwhile Christian members of the team went to ground to pray the whole disaster through, pleading with God to let supernatural wisdom pick a peaceful path through this mine-field.

Mike, having determined since January to drive 06 down the river, was now faced with a huge obstacle. River Rover 06 had been bought by the Highway Trust specifically for Pucallpa. And now the doctor was making dark suggestions about keeping it at San Francisco, and not allowing it to go out of his sight. He wanted Mike to fly to Lima to talk to the lawyers. As we prayed about the crisis, we saw that the key issue to the doctor was the precious medicines. If we relented on that, he might forego his other demands and let us get away.

Mike, Horace and I walked up the steps to meet Julian and the doctor. We gave him his medicines. In order to release 06 to go down river, Mike gave in graciously on almost everything. To have an argument or to allow ourselves the privilege of getting cross would have spelled disaster. 'A soft answer turns away anger,' says the Book of Proverbs, and it proved true again in this case.

The whole affair was a sad finale to the team's memorable stay on the Apurímac. On November 5th, the traditional English ceremony – totally incomprehensible to the Peruvians – was held at Base Camp. In the place of Guy Fawkes burned an effigy in a white coat. The Amazon Trust unfortunately lost a lot of goodwill through the affair, but they certainly gained a lot from our presence. The final preparations for moving were in hand.

Tony Maher had pleaded with me to build more 'excite-ment' into my planning of the down-river journey. Ever the adventurer, he could not bear the idea of the team being shepherded in a giant flock to Pucallpa. He asked me to let the Geminis, the canoe and the River Rover travel independently, meeting at Pucallpa five days later (or however long it would take). That I could not agree to. Instead I set up a rendezvous for each stage of the journey, so that each group could proceed separately, but we would never have a separation of more than about 100 kilometres. Since we were using two-man tents and individual rations, I could also pair up the team on the 'buddy-buddy' principle. That would at least give some independence from the crowd.

I also took the opportunity to pair people up across the boundaries that had developed between the different sections of the team. The two age extremes of the team, Paul Turton and Horace; seasoned sailor Doug and refined Christian doctor David Langley; two strong independent characters, Roy and Dick Bell. Some in the team suspected my sanity or my twisted humour, but the mélange served its purpose.

It was ironic that poor Tony, who had been living for weeks in anticipation of this journey, was one of those struck down by illness. Only days before departure, when he seemed to have recovered, he had to return to his bed. The effort of preparation had been too much and too soon for his body; he had refused to accept that he was so severely weakened.

On the Sunday before departure, Mike arranged a short service at nine a.m. – just to get the whole move into perspective and commit it to God for His protection and blessing. Some of Julian's boys came over with a rocking chair which Julian had given to Mike. They dismantled it in front of him, so that he could see how to 'mantle' it at home.

'We'll have to pay Mike a visit in Herefordshire,' remarked Jim, 'he'll never be able to put that thing together without us.'

We were all going down-river now except Chris and Tim, our super-efficient Base Camp administrators. They were to go on the lorry to Lima, and be responsible for all the equipment that was eventually to be shipped home. I outlined the planned days. We were aiming to take a maximum of six days to cover the 1,000 kilometre journey. The first day was to cover the Rios Apurímac and Ene, camping close to Puerto Ocopa, where we had met President Belaunde a week before. The second day was to finish at Atalaya, where we could get fuel from the nearby Shell Exploration depot.

103

I issued home-made maps of the river – photographs taken from a Shell Exploration satellite map given to us by Paul Turton's father, a radio expert who had spent most of his working life in Peru.

The doctors warned us of some of the dangers of the Amazon region. 'Avoid being bitten by sandflies,' they advised. 'They can carry Leishmaniasin. The bite develops into a tropical sore, and later you develop sores in your eyes and mouth. It is a very serious disease, and this is positively the worst region of the world for it.'

'What's the treatment?' asked someone.

'Well, people have tried antimony,' came the reassuring reply, 'but no one knows whether it works.'

That night we were given one of the only two beautiful sunsets that we had had throughout the whole of our stay in the Apurímac. Purples and greens stretched out over the sky, covering it with an irridescence and glow that warmed our hearts. It was as if God was giving His accolade to the work we had done over the last eight weeks. The purples turned to pink, with streaks of mauve and red flung across them; then the whole thing gradually turned to crimson and died in a reddish gold. Only a few of us saw it through the doors of the ops centre, which were festooned with children, all gawping at us as we enjoyed a farewell party. In Peru one can do nothing in private.

At about seven p.m. some of the team slipped out to church to pay their last sad farewells to the local Christians. The courteous Pastor asked that the greetings of the Church in Peru be taken back with us to Britain. We often pray for the lovely Christian people there, simple in their faith, and poor in their assets.

On the big day, Monday, November 8th, everyone was up at five a.m. to achieve the early start that Mike insisted upon.

On this first day, Dick Bell was in charge of the hovercraft – heavy with equipment and four passengers. As always, everyone in the hovercraft would take it in turns to drive. It was a joy to share this privilege with all on the team. The morning mists clung to the hills. There was more than a touch of drizzle in the air, and the humidity, firmly entrenched in the atmosphere, adding to the heavy breath of the four in the hovercraft, was gumming up the windows. The passengers smeared the droplets from one side to the other in a vain attempt to see out. It was familiar ground. Round the hairpin, bumping down over the rapids by Sivia, now swollen with the last few days' rain, they cavorted over the cross-currents that swirled and eddied into the Apurímac as side-streams flushed their eroded effluent into the main flow.

The weather started to clear up after an hour, as the sun desperately laboured to push its way through the resisting clouds. Mists hanging low over the hills struggled to get up from their weary beds, and the insistent rain was losing its battle with its tropical environment.

Back at San Francisco, we who were to travel in the canoe were looking in dismay at the mountain of freight standing on the riverbank – and wondering impatiently how long a last-minute oil change for the engines would take. By the time we cast off in the pouring rain, it was eight thirty a.m.

In a way I was sad to leave San Francisco, but my main feeling was one of relief that we were actually under way on the long journey.

The terrain gradually cleared as we went north, the hills dropping back to give a better view of the sky. They were always lurking in the background, as if waiting to pounce on unwary strangers or straggling travellers. But they bowed a graceful retreat, giving way to *pampas* plains and Campa frames. The Indian population became more sparse as we went downstream. Fewer clusters of palm-frond huts could be seen poking cheekily above the tall *pampas* reed; fewer dogs barked accusingly at us; fewer children stood at the water's edge, dressed in their stiff, mud-encrusted *cushmas*, to stare. The scenery was beautiful, but became more lonely.

The Geminis worked together as a pair, with Tony and Stuart in charge, but otherwise the various craft worked as three separate units. They moved at their own pace, the only proviso being that none should go past a meeting point until all had arrived there. This at least narrowed the field of search should something go wrong.

On one flat part of the river, where the Geminis and 06 were

105

sharing the same stretch of water, they were visited by Miguel in his Cessna. He buzzed low over them two or three times, and Dick stood up in the hovercraft, with the canopy open, to give him a cheery wave. We had got to know him well, and he had been a good friend throughout the expedition. He flew on in his powerful machine to make one of his regular stops at Quiteni.

So far the river had been wide, winding gently through open terrain. But on the map the river now, ominously, became a thin line. No wide water. No open spaces. Dick and his crew pondered what 'a thin line' could mean in terms of all the water we now saw coursing down the river. They had tackled many fierce rapids above San Francisco; this would be a new experience.

High, vertical cliff edges, standing sheer from the water, rugged and inhospitable, stood as a silent challenge to this new machine, dwarfing it many times over. Some of us had driven through here successfully only a week before. But now it was Dick's turn.

There were no rapids in the gorge. Instead, great buttresses of granite stuck out into the water, causing it to rotate right across their path. The river no longer took up graceful curves, but zig-zagged in a frenzy of indecision. Now flowing left, suddenly flowing right; and at times flowing backwards, ugly and violent. This was a river to be feared.

Dick sensed the challenge. He had met such occasions many times before in his flying days, and thrilled again to dare God to keep them all alive. The others were far less certain.

Turning exultantly to Stu Antrobus, Dick said,

'We really must get a picture of the hovercraft going through this gorge. Grab your cine, and let's see what we can do.' A chorus of disagreement met him. But as they rounded the next bend, they saw a convenient rock jutting out from the edge.

'Come on. Let's stop there and let Stu off. He can climb up the cliff and get a vertical photo of the hovercraft sweeping round the bend.'

Turning round in the river, Dick slowed the hovercraft down and into the water like a boat. As he coasted gently up to the rocks, Stu and James leapt out, slipping and skidding on the wet, mossy surface. Gingerly they scrambled up the rocky

106

crags, hanging on to any bit of foliage they could find, until they had reached a perch high enough to take a good photograph.

The hovercraft pushed off to tackle this exciting whirlpool-infested gorge again. After all, if it had coped with it twice, it could go on coping for evermore. And it did. Sturdy, responsive, and stable, it flew sweetly over anything that would be death to a raft, disaster to a bad canoe, and danger to the Geminis.

At four thirty p.m., we in the canoe came across the hovercraft crew trying to set up a radio aerial on a beach. That was the time I had fixed with the Embassy for a radio call each day, but the radio contact on that particular Monday was poor, and the messages were garbled.

Mike took the canoe on to find a camp site for the night. The place he found was at the river confluence, level, but also apparently the main cattle highway to the river. There were some of them still around, and many other obvious signs of their passing! Cattle meant bugs. Nurse Louise went round ordering us to wear long-sleeved clothing, as malaria had not been eradicated here. A bonfire was soon blazing, and the resourceful James returned to his favourite pastime, brewing hot chocolate. It was all a little experimental on this first night. The plea for adventure, and independent camping, became meaningless as the team were drawn like insects to the bonfire.

Dick Ball and I had rearranged the seats in the hovercraft as beds, and with mosquito netting sealing the open canopy we spent a comfortable night. But in the tents they sweltered. Lying in their underwear, totally enclosed, with little rivers of perspiration running down their backs, on uneven and lumpy cow-dung, some found sleep elusive. At least the mosquitos didn't get in!

We broke camp brighter and earlier than the dawn to spend half an hour getting the canoe floating. At five a.m. Mike Cole had found it aground; the river had dropped two feet in the night.

We ate our porridge and apricot flakes, drank our hot tea, and dismantled our tents. The little nibblers had discovered us again. They had probably been searching all night for some good human flesh to get stuck into.

We would wait for the Geminis to turn up before we set off

down the Rio Tambo. When they had failed to arrive the previous day, we assumed that they had made camp up-river.

They came in at seven thirty, unkempt and unwashed. Earlier problems with Tony's 55 hp engine had persisted, and Stu Forbes, the other Gemini leader, had stayed behind to soldier along with him. They had had to hold the engine together with finger and string for the whole 60-mile journey.

At four p.m. they found themselves right in the throat of the Ene gorge. Its jaws had opened up for them, and they struggled valiantly with its swirling rotations, only to have yet another engine failure right in the middle. They limped to the edge where there was a narrow but very welcome sandbank. There they decided to spend the night. There was hardly room to put the tents up, and no substantial trees to which to tie the inflatables, but they used the remaining one and a half hours of daylight to fix the annoying accelerator rod with Araldite, and allowed it to dry overnight. It never gave any more trouble. The Gemini crews were up at five to leave that terrifying gorge as quickly as they could.

We were now all on unknown territory. The Rio Tambo turns almost immediately south-east, flowing in that direction for quite a number of kilometres. After that it turns north again, and I gave our next meeting point as Poyeni, a town large enough to be named on all the maps. Thereafter we would make for Atalaya and for the Shell depot to buy fuel. I would captain the hovercraft today.

The pairing up of the team was already starting to cause trouble. It had seemed natural to put the two girls together, but now Cathy was suffering. Her face was puffed up from the effects of the relentless sun during the previous day. Dick Bell made representations for her to have a day in the shade, and I put her and Louise on the hovercraft crew for at least the first half of the day. But Louise didn't like that idea. She thought that the Gemini would be a much more exciting means of travel.

With an eye on the chaos which would result if pairs were split up to meet every individual's desires, I became stubborn. The girls would be with Ricardo and me in the hovercraft until Poyeni.

The Geminis were the first away, thirty minutes ahead, with

Stu 'Phot' aboard to find a vantage point for cine of the hovercraft going through the Tambo gorge. We yet had to see what that was like. The canoe was last.

We had often queried in our minds the oddity of naming one continuous stretch of water Apurímac-Ene-Tambo-Ucayali-Amazon. But we began to see the cause as we whined our way down between its sheer banks. President Belaunde called the Tambo the 'Elbow of the Amazon'. It is the only lengthy bit of this 3,500-mile river that has any southerly flow. That southerly bend is the beginning of the new river and the new name, the Rio Tambo.

It was the environment that changed the character. We had seen a gorge in the Rio Ene, boiling and swirling and curling with its gaping whirlpools. But practically the whole of the Rio Tambo is a gorge, although not in the sense that the sheer cliffs run vertically into the torrent. In the Tambo they often stand back from the edge to allow half a kilometre of Amazon forest to live out its precarious existence. The straggly trees, topped with dark green and supported by spindly trunks, push their urgent toupees up to catch the glistening sunshine. What space there is between the river bank and the cliff bottom is jammed with flora and forest, bramble and banana, leaf and stem, as if they were constantly in contention with the rest of the world for the privilege of breathing.

I had been apprehensive about this stretch. From the camp site we could see the terrain narrowing, the hills crowding in to squeeze the flowing water into the gorge. Julian had warned us about it, telling of the powerful and complex currents. This was where he had crashed on a balsa raft, when he and John Ridgway had dared to challenge the mighty river. They had been stuck for three days without water or food, eaten alive by voracious mosquitos, and clinging precariously to a crumbling island next to the yawning vortex of a whirlpool. By God's grace, some Campa Indians discovered them and rescued them.

The River Rover, however, skimmed scornfully over the smooth surface of the water, as if laughing at the swirling underwater currents. I stayed at the controls, in wary anticipation. Forty-five minutes slipped by. We had sailed effortlessly past

109

the island that had been both Julian's downfall and his lifeline so many years before. Still we waited for trouble.

Then Louise innocently burst the bubble.

'When do we get to this gorge, then?' she asked. My wariness melted away as I realised that the gorge held no more mysteries. Or at least none that were likely to harm us.

Once we found a beach to land on, Louise took the controls for her first hovercraft 'driving lesson'. Within a few minutes she had mastered the basics of controlling direction and holding a steady speed. Cathy dozed off in the back, reclaiming some of the sleeping time lost the previous night. While Louise concentrated on the driving, Dick Ball and I lapsed into silence, welcoming the opportunity just to look around, to observe what those in the canoe could observe all the time.

The cloud covered our sky as we growled downstream. For the most part, the tops of the hills were covered in irregular sine waves, as the mists dripped their beads of moisture on to the jungle foliage. Here and there, the trees surrendered their burden of moisture, and cloud rose from the steaming jungle, forming a necklace of pearl round the crest of the hills, slowly rising to embrace its mother at the top. As bend after bend was rounded new patterns of cloud emerged: now strings of pearls; now diamond tiaras; now clusters of pearls and diamonds set in emerald and jade.

There were cliffs, unusual for the rivers we had seen. It was as if the Tambo was a gigantic earthquake crack that had suddenly subsided five hundred feet. The hills were, in part, overgrown. But here, more than anywhere else on the river complex, were the sheer walls of geological fault towering above us like the battlements of some medieval castle. In places it looked manufactured, as if some long-forgotten king had built a fortress to stave off the attacks of his foes. Pillars, colonnades, turrets and towers rose in majesty. In places the mortar had decayed and the building had crumbled, and large square chunks of rock tilted precariously from gaping holes. All along it creepers clung to the little fissures; bushes dared to venture existence, and the occasional skinny tree lurched drunkenly from the sheer face, swaying unsteadily in the breeze.

To the eye of fear, or to those who had no faith to see beyond the surface, the Rio Tambo was inhospitable, domineering or boring. To those who could see a Creator's genius, and were ready to be taught a Creator's matchless excellence, the Rio Tambo vibrated with a spectacular drama.

It was, perhaps, the poorest area we had seen for human life. Just two canoes passed us on this 7½-kilometre stretch before the elbow at Poyeni turned us north again. The few people who lived by its banks were Campa Indians. We had seen poor Campas before, but nearly all we had seen had been touched by civilisation in some way. This part of the Rio Tambo was the most unsophisticated we saw throughout the whole 1,000 kilometres.

There were few signs even of Campa canoes. Certainly, the most noticeable feature of the Campa life here was that there was no cultivation. No banana plantations. No plantains. They knew enough to hack down the dense undergrowth and build their palm-leaf shelters on spindly stilts. Certainly, with those insurmountable hills towering behind, there would be no road. Or, it seemed, even paths. There were no signs of animals. Not one dog barked at our passing.

There are those who say that the aboriginal tribes should be left alone, that the influence of civilisation can only be bad. And yet this very hovercraft, 06, would return to the Rio Tambo. The Christian Church in Peru would use it to bring new life, both physical and spiritual, to these and other tribes of the jungle. They argued that civilisation was, in any case, making its inexorable advance into the *selva*. Oil exploration was bringing whole new towns, with air conditioning, Coca-Cola and pop music. If the tribes were to be influenced, said the churches, let it be for good.

At last came the first glimmerings of a change. First a cow and some scraggy maize. Then a Western T-shirt. Then a fruit tree. Then a group of canoes. Then the steep overbearing crags giving way to gentler slopes, to more room near the river, to more open terrain. It felt as if we were emerging into dawn from a long hard night. The grey overcast still remained, but because the hills had retreated and humbled themselves, more light shone in. It was like a new spring. A new breath of good clean air.

111

The river turned north. The hills fell away and disappeared altogether. We passed more and more settlements, each one increasing its signs of cultivation until we passed a fairly large tributary on the right-hand side flanked by a high bank about thirty feet above the surface of the river. There were houses on top; some enterprising soul had cut steps in the mud bank all the way up. We discovered later that this was Poyeni, our planned R.V.[1], but we continued past it.

Poyeni marked the tip of the finger of civilisation stretched at arm's length up river. Boca del Mantaro is its counterpart on the finger stretched down river from San Francisco and Sivia. The river Ene gets bleaker and bleaker as it heads for the darkness of the Tambo. And that part of the Tambo inside those cliffs is, so far as our experience took us, the blackest, most uninhabited, and barest part of the whole Amazon. Not even our detailed map showed any village names on the elbow of the Amazon.

The others never had any difficulty seeing the hovercraft by the side of the river. It shimmered in the heat and its white canopy could be seen for miles. The canoe was always last in the race to get to the R.V.s. I apologised that we had missed Poyeni! We had found this flat but very soft stretch of sand. Tea was already brewing for the last of the team, who were glad to emerge from the confines of the canoe.

The housing style was changing. The normal Campa houses were open-sided and roofed with palm leaves. Now we saw houses which made much greater use of the abundant wood with which the Amazon jungle is blessed. The roofs were still the same, but now there were also wooden walls to keep out the worst of the monsoon winds and rains. Occasionally, the bright gleam of a corrugated-iron roof sparkled at the river's edge.

There were no rapids from now on. The fall had reduced to two inches per mile, and the slow sluggish mass of water, like Old Man River, just kept rolling along. No longer was the turbulence too awful to contemplate, as it had been on the 'Great Speaker'. Now a mighty flood of unstoppable liquid carried all before it. You cannot fight the Amazon. You have to succumb, and do things its way.

[1] *R.V.*: rendezvous.

112

Awaiting the hover doctor

Stuart Forbes uses his strong spanner wrist to good effect

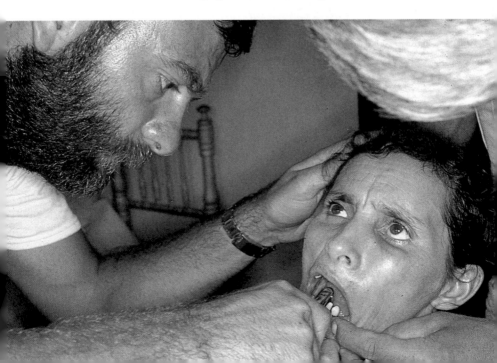

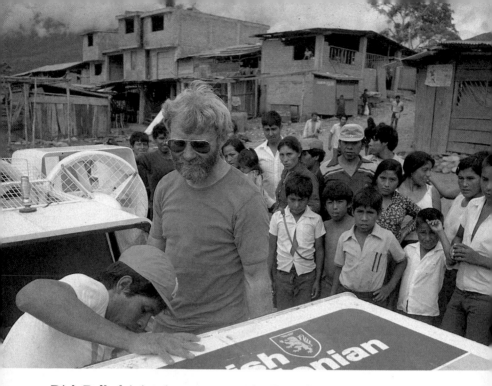

Dick Bell, driving instructor to the Peruvians

Quechua mother

Campa chief, Amadeo, with his family

Peter Dixon and Mike Cole meet President Belaúnde

Gemini en route to Pucallpa

President Belaúnde enjoys River Rover

As we progressed we saw more and more riverside dwellings. People had begun to part the trees, raping and massacring this impenetrable jungle with fire, saw, axe and sweat, to build their little paradises beside the 'motorway'. Grassy banks and lawns appeared as we drew close to Atalaya. Stone or block buildings gradually became more frequent. The shores of the Amazon were being tamed.

One of the indistinct messages that we had received from the British Embassy the previous night was that we should avoid Atalaya township. We were uncertain why. 'To avoid red tape' was what they said. But the implication was that we would be suspected of drug-running.

As the various craft separately made their northward progress, those in the open boats had a thorough soaking from a passing tropical storm. The hovercraft had different problems. Dick Ball, the indomitable Ricardo, was learning something about headwind techniques as I watched. He had taken the helm for the final leg to the Shell depot and now, perhaps, he was regretting it. For with the rain the storm had brought wind. He had to hold the craft hard against the right bank – sneaking under overhanging trees, weaving in and out of the clumps of accumulated driftwood.

Atalaya appeared on the left bank, now a good mile away. The presence of many boats, and a plane approaching to land, confirmed that it was the right place. We need not have bothered checking. Just past the township, on the starboard side, the river widened out into what looked like a lake. We had found the mouth of the Rio Urubamba.

The Urubamba rises to the south of Cuzco. Later some of us would ride the railway along the river's winding bank to visit the ruined city of Machu Picchu. The river twists its turbulent way past that awesome Inca eyrie, through Machiguenga Indian territory, until it joins its sister the Tambo to become the Rio Ucayali. The volume of water from the Urubamba was about the same as that from the Tambo – immense. We wondered what this extraordinary river was like further north, when so much water was flowing into it here. We were told that 200-ton coasters regularly came up to Atalaya.

Resisting the temptation to investigate Atalaya, the first

113

town we had seen in two days, we turned up the Urubamba to search for the Shell depot at Maldonadillo. A boat passed us going the other way. They seemed to sit very low in the water. 'Heavily laden,' we thought. But no. We passed another. And then it clicked; because there were no rapids here at all, the two-foot sides on our canoe were unnecessary. These boats chugged past with a very novel engine system; a Japp four-stroke motor, the sort one would find on a rotavator or other small agricultural machine in England, driving a propeller at the end of a long tube. The whole engine could be turned to give direction, and the tiller could be pushed down to clear the propeller from any debris that might get entangled in it. We later learned that the ingenious, simple boats were called *peci-pecis*; the onomatopoeic name suited them perfectly.

After about fifteen minutes, the Shell symbol on a signboard confirmed that we had the right location, and Ricardo made a very creditable landing on an awkward little track leading up from the river.

But the Shell Exploration workers had not heard of us, even though Frank Turton had sent on a message about the expedition. Giving us coffee, they called up their main exploration base by radio to ask if they could sell us the 200 gallons we were asking for. They, too, knew nothing.

The next step was a call to Lima. By now, of course, we were beginning to worry. Back came the reply from Shell Lima, frustratingly relayed through the third party. 'Yes,' they said, 'give them the petrol.' Give. Yes, give. Free. Frank Turton had turned up trumps for us. All day Mike Cole had been praying that we would get our planned – but very uncertain – refuel without difficulty. The radio message was his answer.

We made haste to empty the stocks we had in the canoe into the Geminis and hovercraft, and then rolled the four 45-gallon drums clumsily off the canoe in exchange for four full ones. With considerable grunting and heaving, and with great difficulty, we transferred these weighty drums to their new home.

It was three thirty p.m. and time to move on. What, didn't they have any hotels for us to spend the night in? No one asked. We were on an expedition, and wanted to taste every hardship imaginable. There were plenty of those!

CHAPTER NINE

Creeping Up

WHEN WE LEFT the oil exploration depot, not much daylight remained. I led the little convoy back down the Urubamba to the confluence in search of a camp site for the night. Suitable for the combined needs of boats and hovercraft, large enough for all of the tents; the ideal camp site was something we had not yet come across. And this time we did not want to travel much further.

From the confluence we sped downstream for about a mile, and then spied some open flat land, unusual for that area, on the opposite bank about a mile away. As we came closer, it showed itself as an island, about 300 metres in length. The hovercraft slid smoothly on to the flat, even sand. There were no bushes, only a few reeds on the downstream end. As the Geminis and the canoe settled easily on to the shallow beach, the calm water quietly lapping at their hulls, their occupants clambered happily out, lugging the two-man tents on their backs. Here was the night's five-star luxury.

Soon the encampment was complete, the neat Vango tents standing in a row, on the highest ground but still only a few feet above water level. I had issued one Millbank purifying bag between two. There are more sophisticated methods of filtering water, but the Millbank is unbeatable. Just pour the muddy brown river water in, catch the clean water dripping from the bag, and pop in a chlorine tablet. In ten minutes, clean water. Soon Roy brought his engineering common sense to work. A row of bags hung over a length of aluminium channel (a hovercraft spare), a jerrycan under the end of the channel, and we had a centralised water supply. From such ingenuity was civilisation born.

Our radio contact with the Embassy that afternoon was the last good one of the journey, a fact we were later dearly to regret. But that was days ahead.

It was a short night's sleep. By ten thirty, Ricardo Ball and I were awake, listening to the sound of lapping water around three sides of the craft. Ricardo shone a torch out into the darkness, searching for the rock we had marked in an earlier moment of suspicion, at the edge of the water. It was half submerged. We held a quick two-man conference. Would the river keep rising, continuing to respond to the rains of days before, hundreds of miles away in the mountains?

Now the River Rover was surrounded by water, and a move was called for. Ricardo held the powerful searchlight under the overcast night sky, while I shattered the stillness with the sound of turning fans. I drove up the barely discernible incline and dumped the craft unceremoniously less than a metre from the tent shared by Brian Holdsworth and Tony Maher. Later I learned that Tony had not even woken up.

By eleven thirty it was obvious that the inexorable rise had not reached its zenith. Roy had, by now, emerged from the darkness, and the three of us patrolled the encampment, watching the water creep closer. We woke the occupants of the outlying tents, trying to give them just enough time before they were cut off.

Midnight was decision time. 'Come on, wake up,' we shouted as we unzipped tent doorways, 'this is your practice early morning call.' Within fifteen minutes the camp was struck, each person had instructions on where to go when there was no more dry land, and people were lying down on the ground again to grab some sleep before the inevitable occurred. Hexamine stoves appeared.

'If this is morning,' said Doug, 'we'd better have breakfast.' So out came the porridge, to add some sanity to the new day.

The river kept rising. Soon most of the team were bedded down in the canoe or the Geminis. Ricardo and I moved the hovercraft on to the higher ground, where the tents had been. The faint moonlight, struggling to illuminate the jungle through shifting layers of cloud, conspired with the river to play tricks on the mind. As the changing currents around the former island drifted the boats this way and that, it was hard to establish any fixed frame of reference against the moving surface of the water.

In the canoe Paul Turton, sitting in the bows, noticed that they were drifting. The rope had become untied, and the boat was moving gently through the tops of the reeds, which had now been partly covered by the rising water.

'Let it drift,' said Mike. 'It can only take us downstream, where we want to go. Go to sleep.'

Tired, aching, and full of pins and needles, the team slept fitfully, grousing when anyone turned over and rocked the boat. In the hovercraft we were awake all night, starting it up three times to reposition it as the dry land contracted, and covering the other boats with spray. Although the hovercraft will float, it does not float well, and the odd leak or two in the hull would bode ill for the craft if it were to stay in the water for any length of time.

Eventually the first glimmerings of grey light started to draw the indistinct tree line into a more solid boundary between the Amazon jungle and the heavy overcast. As the water became visible I started up the hovercraft. It was five a.m. With a roar, we were off on a new day's adventure.

The canoe was second. There really wasn't any point in staying there any longer. So much for the idyllic five-star hotel. The whole sandbank had disappeared. A conservative estimate would say that the water had risen one metre overnight. There are no tides there – not at 2,500 miles from the sea. The rain in the hills must have been torrential to produce so much water in such a short time. And the river here was at least half a mile wide.

Canoe travel on the river at that hour of the morning was hazardous. Maxi sat, as he had for days, cross-legged at the front of the canoe, signalling manfully to Horacio to go left, go right, pull the outboards in, as if he were conducting Beethoven. There was no way that he could communicate by voice above the noise of the two motors. The whole surface of the water was littered with debris from fish traps, houses by the riverside, and with all the cast-off junk that man throws away throughout the year. At the Shell Depot, they said that they had not really had any rain up to that point. So here it was. And it was a mess. One cannot prevent the river pulling trees and bushes into its flow by erosion. But one can feel ashamed at man's selfishness and thoughtlessness in not disposing of his garbage in a sensible way. Is it so different in 'civilised' countries?

With a crunch, the canoe hit something. Horacio stopped both motors, and pulled them up. Ruefully he looked at a propeller that was buckled and broken. They could continue on one engine. But they couldn't move on that propeller.

We were fortunate that this expedition had a wise, prayerful and shrewd leader. For weeks we had fought to conserve our stocks of engine spares, and we had seemed to be down to the bottom of the barrel. But Mike had brought a spare prop. He hadn't told anyone. He realised that if anyone knew that there was a spare prop around, he would not be as careful as if he thought he already had the last. Mike unearthed the prop from amongst his socks and shirts, and the engineers set about fitting it.

Barely delayed, they roared back into the chase again. The Geminis drew level with the canoe, anxious to catch it up, straining to overtake. Every now and then people pondered the thought of breakfast, but forgot it. Just munch a bit of chocolate or a dextrose tablet. In any case, breakfast had been at midnight for most of us. What's a lost meal under the circumstances? It's not even hardship. Neither could it be regarded as hardship to have had little sleep, to be wet and cold, to be bitten by mosquitos of inexpressible ferocity, to go without a wash for two days. Adventure was what we were here for!

Just as the Tambo had been different from the Ene, so the Ucayali was different again. It was now about a mile wide. Fortunately, the logs and twigs and huge great tree trunks that were turning over slowly in the water and floating lazily down river, were drawn to the place of maximum current. They tended to be in a line, holding to the left or the right of the river, as the flow dictated. This eased things for the canoe and inflatables considerably.

The riverside habitations became increasingly interesting.

We passed a magnificent estate that we could only think was a Mission station. A neat, circular house, capped by a 'Noddy' roof, was the centrepiece. A stepped concrete path cut an artistic walkway down to the river's edge through a well-kept lawn. The lawn itself extended over the whole of the grounds, rising and falling over the humps as if it had been landscaped. Other lawns were at different levels and some boasted summer houses. Beds of tropical flowers could be glimpsed through the fence that surrounded the property. Other permanent buildings were grouped farther inland. It was very beautiful, like the Mission at Puerto Ocopa; it showed what can be done by someone who has a vision for design, and the energy to put it into action.

The whole of the Amazon area is wild and raw in its natural state, but can be made into a tropical paradise by someone with drive. It has the two essential ingredients for fruitfulness – sunshine and water. What a challenge it would be for a keen young man to cut down the forest and tame it, to plant grass, and to grow those beautiful, fragrant tropical flowers and trees. And to earn a good living by selling the produce: fruit, vegetables and animals. Very few people in a Western society can influence their nation by more than a fraction of a per cent. But in Peru, or in any other developing nation, any improvement is a major step forward and can be satisfyingly enjoyed. After all, Julian has helped the Apurímac valley to achieve in a decade what Western nations have taken centuries to do in their own countries. What a challenge to take up!

Later that morning, the canoe's motors cut. Horacio shrugged his shoulders in a *mañana* way. After some debate, it transpired that he had no spare plugs. Nor, for that matter, did he have any of the correct spanners with which to fix it. On the Apurímac, Aurelio had invariably fixed the outboards with a bit of wood, a rock, and sometimes a bit of wire. The condition of the engines told the tale. Horacio seemed to be one of the same breed. He pulled out a bit of bent metal and was about to start work on hammering the plug out when Mike stopped him. Digging into his socks and shirts again, he produced a plug and a bag of Johnson spanners – the right ones for these motors.

Those were perhaps the best moments to be sitting in the

119

canoe. The boat drifted down the muddy river, hissing slightly as it rubbed against sand or debris. With no roaring engines to disturb the peace, the sounds were like poetry. The gentle lapping of the water on the hull complemented the song of the Amazon. Only a fully mature forest could chant like that.

Somehow the soul of man could be knit with the soul of the Creator in this setting. It was deeply enriching, totally fulfilling for the heart that wanted to find peace and contentment. The sun's warmth was gentle, and fleecy clouds meandered lazily under a canopy of azure. If only those we loved at home could just come and share its excellence with us!

By the time the Geminis and the weary canoe group reached the first R.V. of the day, Chicosa, we in the hovercraft had been there for an hour. The machine perched at a drunken angle on the flimsiest of verges. Places where the hovercraft could easily beach were now becoming hard to find.

The team disembarked, stretching stiff legs and untangling aching arms, woolly-mouthed, greasy-faced, empty-bellied and thirsty. Toothbrushes whirred into action, and the muddy river collected a bit more filth from dishevelled explorers.

The Chicosa people came out to see the hovercraft; even the school broke up for an hour to see this thing that had miraculously appeared on their front doorstep. They were Campas, but not the Campas we knew up-river, dressed in their *cushmas* and living Stone-Age lives. These were all dressed in Western-type clothing, trousers and T-shirts, and the girls in dresses of different colours. They all spoke Spanish, even the little ones, as well as their own native Campa tongue. Educated, well turned out, civilised, transformed. We could hardly believe that they came from the same tribe.

Dick Bell, especially, was thinking back to those other Campas we had grown to love, somewhere back up the river. They, too, could be well fed, have good medical care, and be well-educated, by God's grace. And what a glorious hope for those poor pathetic villages in the dark and deserted Tambo. Big-hearted, enthusiastic, compassionate Dick. He had spent so much of his life praying for people. And he had found that a strange thing happens when you pray for people; you get involved with them. Whether it's acknowledged or not, people

120

who pray form a bond with those they pray for. Even when the
hands are helpless, the hearts are not.

Dick and Roy picked up a pair of doctors, abandoned the
rest of us to canoe and Geminis, and rode out in style in the
hovercraft. Close to the bank at Chicosa was the line of floating
logs that marked the main stream. The hovercraft, avoiding the
protrusions that would tear a finger or two in the skirt, sailed
smoothly and disdainfully over the rest, and droned its way
across the open water into the hazy morning.

Looking at the map, it seemed that navigation could become
difficult. We had already discovered that the mapped location
of villages did not always tie up with the inhabitants' opinions
on where they lived. The confusion was augmented by the
curves in the river. Some that were shown did not exist, and
others that were not shown did. This river changed its course
from month to month; and our map could only show the
situation on a given date. Until Chicosa, the map had tallied
with reality, but this was no longer true.

The river wriggled onward like a trapped anaconda. Islands
appeared in the middle of the river. At times what appeared
to be the shortest way down river ended in a cul-de-sac and
Dick had to turn about and retrace his path. The larger islands
were so Amazonically huge that it wasn't hard to lose bearings
altogether. At one they never saw the real river, and found
themselves travelling south-east. They had gone all the way
round an island without realising it. Roy brought his nautical
common sense to bear. 'Only travel,' he said, 'where the flow at
the bank is down river.' So simple, yet so necessary. Often the
direction of flow was clear only at the extreme edge of the
broad swathe of water.

The doctors drove the hovercraft, enjoying the exciting but
exacting experience in the beautiful morning. Crystal clear
skies stretched out, dark blue overhead changing imperceptibly
into light aquamarine at the horizon.

Mile after mile of green trees and the vast tranquil river
etched themselves for ever on our memories. Large kingfishers
skimmed the surface of the water like a hovercraft, climbing
up and diving into the murkiness as their keen eyes spotted a
tasty lunch. They were larger than the kingfishers in Britain,

121

aquamarine and ruddy brown underneath and glistening black on top, with a magnificent crest that justified their royal title. Butterflies navigated crazily across the river. Herons stood in the shallows by the water's edge, still as Nelson's column, with their dagger beaks ready to spear some unsuspecting fish. There were three kinds of heron. The normal European grey heron was fairly common, as were the white herons. They stood out at the riverside like neon lights on an unlit road, and we saw a number of mating pairs. The last version of heron was a Giant Grey, an unreal blow-up of the Common, as if God had given it hormone tablets for a year, or fed it on steak and eggs every day. It lunged into the air as the hovercraft sped past.

The water in the vast shallow tracts on the inside of bends was as smooth as glass, and often barely an inch deep. The hovercraft skimmed over its glassy calm, leaving little trace of its passing. It's the mark of every thoroughbred: courageously ploughing through the difficult tasks, and suavely enjoying the rest.

In places, the tall reeds that usually dominated the banks fell away, and lighter marsh grass edged the river. Plainly, the high-water season would expand the river into a lake, covering the spikey leaves that grew out of the mud. But now they made for good sport. River Rover 06 wove in and out of them, cutting the corners of the huge bends, and often riding right over the top. The doctors were at first fearful of flying over the reed grass; after all, it's not something that is ever done in a boat. But they became more confident of the hovercraft characteristics as they proved its ability. The reeds might not have been there! At one point, the reed grass grew quite a way out into the river by a village. Local Indians were slowly paddling their shallow dug-outs through them to their fish traps, quite a hive of activity both ashore and on the river. The hovercraft passed them on the inside, swerving in and out of the reeds and traps with cheery waves to the fishermen. They had never seen anything like this before.

The hovercraft was the first to arrive at Bolognesi, our planned resting-place for the night. The time? Ten thirty-five a.m., just two hours away from Chicosa. Dick found a spot for the machine down river from the town centre, on a shallow edge of grass outside someone's front garden.

The lady owner of the house had no objections: indeed, she was flattered. An ostentatious Peruvian zoomed up in his aluminium boat, showing off his 50 hp Suzuki outboard. He parked deftly, and got out to examine his rival. A large crowd had gathered and Dick, ever the enthusiast, did his best in his now superb pidgin Spanish to sell the hovercraft idea to everybody. Performance, control, engine, petrol consumption, load-carrying capacity, even hovercraft principles – their thirst for knowledge was insatiable!

Later, David Langley and Dick went round the grounds of the house, asking questions about everything they saw. The lady had lived there for thirty years, and the house was already built when she came to it. It stood one metre high on stilts, indicating a river rise of three metres or so. The river itself was nearly a mile across at this point, so the amount of water that torrented down the Ucayali in the wet season must be phenomenal. They looked around at the garden and the fencing.

'How far does the water go inland?'

'*Lejos*,' the lady said, casually waving her hand in an expansive way. 'Miles.'

'What happens to your garden?'

'It disappears.'

'How do you travel to the town to get your shopping?'

'By boat,' she replied, indicating a couple of battered dug-outs lying nearby.

'And school? Do the children go to school the same way in the rains?'

'Yes. Every day. But it is only two months. Then we get back to normal.'

The two visitors were amazed at the complete change of lifestyle that had to take place within the year. Perhaps it was no more than the change between an English summer and winter, but it certainly seemed like it.

Turning round, David noticed a large dark green-leafed tree standing a few metres from the house, about seven metres high.

123

'Is the fruit edible?' he asked, ever keen to sample the Amazon to its full.

'Certainly,' a man said. 'Try it.' He took a large pole, and despite the abundance of fruit there was on the ground, knocked a bunch from the tree. The fruit was red in colour and grew in groups of about six, all over the tree, mainly towards the tips of the branches. It was the size of a plum, the flesh white, and it had a large stone in the centre. The crispness was that of an apple, the consistency that of a slightly unripe peach, and the flavour was reminiscent of a slightly sour cherry. There was an alcoholic tang to it. The Shipibos called it a Mamaya tree, and laughed at the wry faces as David and Dick sampled it, skin and all. The two also admired a beautiful English rose in the garden, pink and fragrant. It was the first any of us had seen on this side of the Andes.

The two had just finished their tour when the Shipibos warned that rain was on the way. As the huge obliterating sheet of grey approached, the rain sent ahead a warning, like an express train's whistle. A minor roar indicated that it had reached the corrugated iron roofs of the town. Then a deeper, all-pervading roll of a thousand timpani told them that it had reached the banana plantation. The sound, coming from every direction, was alarming. Two courteous drops of rain in warning and then, bang – saturation in twenty seconds. The four bolted for the hovercraft. The locals had taken cover under the trees, showing better forward planning.

Meanwhile the rest of us had arrived in the Geminis and canoe, with not even the luxury of a canopy to shelter us from the downpour. Once Dick had brought 06 back to the tiny inlet to float alongside the canoe for refuelling, we dashed to an incongruous gazebo for a bedraggled conference. We were still not used to the different river conditions, and it had suddenly become difficult to judge how far we could get in a given time. The different speeds and shallow-water capabilities of the four craft made the task even more awkward. We decided to move on to Sempaya for our night stop.

Every eye in the village watched our movements with the keenness of Sherlock Holmes. I found myself siphoning petrol into the hovercraft's tanks, trying not to gag on the all too familiar flavour. We were unsure about some green-tinted petrol that filled one of the drums collected at Atalaya. We put some in the hovercraft, and topped up with yellow petrol, the colour we most enjoyed. Dick said he would test it out. We put only a little in one tank, so that he could change tanks if it turned out to be paraffin or turps; or perhaps even crème de menthe? The engine did not stop so we assumed it to be the real stuff.

We bade farewell to Bolognesi at twelve fifteen and the hovercraft arrived at Sempaya, according to Dick's meticulous records, at two forty-seven. The canoe made more leisurely progress. We saw Indian huts, and sometimes whole villages, half submerged by some change in the river's path, but not destroyed. The river banks here, where there were edges, were clay mud only about a foot or two high. Certainly, there was a tide mark on the base of the trees where water had obviously been. But the rise in water level here seemed to be much less than the 2 to 2½ metres that was characteristic of the Apurímac. So, what happens to all the water? If it doesn't go upwards, it must go outwards. Presumably the mile width that we were now often seeing could easily extend to four or five.

The Amazon has been described as the world's most complex river system. It is much more than that. It dominates. It is the totalitarian dictator of this part of the globe. Woe betide the person who dares to challenge the Amazon without the knowledge of a greater power with him and beside him. The experiences of Werner Herzog, the German film director, come to mind. He was on the Apurímac and Urubamba making the film *Fitzcarraldo* in May 1982, and suffered the most awful difficulties. Later we heard what he thought of the area we had come to love and respect.

This is an unforgiving country, full of potential disaster. There is danger lurking around every corner. The birds don't sing; they screech and cry out in pain. If I believed in the devil, I would say he was right here. Five of my people lost their lives in the aircraft crash, and my cast has changed many times over, because they can't stand this awful country. It is evil, shrieking in pain. There is discord everywhere you go. There is no growth. No order. Even the stars are a mess.

125

There is no harmony in this part of the universe. I love the jungle, but I love it against my better judgment. God, if there is a God, created the jungle in anger. He never finished it, and has not seen it as it is. He abandoned it to its own fate.

It is the view of a man fighting the Amazon on his own.

Everything in the Amazon is bigger and better, more vicious and more violent than, perhaps, anywhere else in the world. But it is also more beautiful, more fragrant, and richer in natural resources than anywhere else in the world. It needs men big enough to tackle it, and small enough to humble themselves under a big God.

The 'principal port' of Sempaya was a muddy bank two feet high, leading to a narrow path that disappeared into the tall straggly riverside reeds. Whatever it looked like, we felt welcome.

The Geminis arrived first. Now that the river had become wide and calm, the hovercraft had no speed advantage over the pair of inflatables. Tony Maher and Stuart Forbes revelled in their new ascendancy. Stuart and his crew rooted around to find a place for 06, and unearthed the mouth of a stream 30 metres away, from which most of the reeds had been cut, and which boasted a bank that actually sloped down to the water. They were soon marshalling the hovercraft into it.

Meanwhile Cathy, who had been on a Gemini, went to find the village. The path took her through a yucca plantation to a stream. It was too wide to cross, and she discovered by poking with a convenient reed that it was too deep to wade through. There were two boats, though. One was a tiny dug-out canoe, the other a covered *peci-peci* with *HOSPITAL AMAZONICA* boldly emblazoned on the side. It seemed only natural to clamber aboard and punt across the 3-metre stream. The village – large, well spread, with substantial wooden houses built on piles – was another 200 metres beyond. Cathy's Spanish had blossomed from nothing to the comprehensible in two months; no matter that every fourth word was a French one. She was always understood. She found the *sanitario* who took her to the *jefe*, the village chief. He in turn had no objections

126

to our camping by the yucca plantation, providing we didn't molest it. Cathy returned triumphant.

In the canoe we arrived about an hour later to find things well ordered, although setting up a radio aerial to contact the Embassy had proved too difficult.

Then they came. It was as if the siren had blown in a factory at knock-off time. Nasty, vicious, voracious, unmerciful: mosquitos. The biggest plague we ever met. They must have smelt the fresh blood, we wagered. The team rushed to put on long-sleeved clothes. Some delved into their rucksacks to trace their jungle hats and face nets, emerging like a posse of beekeepers. I resorted to my heavy waterproof with the hood up and drawstrings tightened, preferring to sweat in the sultry atmosphere rather than to suffer the ministrations of our new enemy. As I prepared a meal, only my hands were uncovered, and next day they were covered by a mass of red weals. The insects even bit through denim jeans. One unfortunate had a shin bite that was still festering four months later.

We decided to call it a day. The best thing to do was to retire gracefully, and think through another strategy at leisure.

The following day, prevented from leaving early by a small repair needed on the hovercraft, we learned a little more about where we were. The village was populated by Shipibo and Conibo Indians, and there were over 600 families living in the *sanitario*'s area. There were three school teachers, one taking the pre-schoolchildren from age three, and the other two teaching the six- to eighteen-year-olds. One of these teachers also took an after-school adult class for those who could not read or write. The Ministry of Education paid for all the schooling. It sounded very well organised.

The Shipibos are different again from their near cousins, the Campas. They look similar, having more mongoloid features, but to the *gringo* eye at least, are not so attractive. The ladies dress in skirts and blouses, unlike the Campa *cushmas*, and the pattern of weave in their cloth is as unique as their language. It is colourful, but not as vivid or gay as the Quechua *mantas*. The pattern is a series of superimposed squares, resembling a patchwork made up of architects' blue-prints. The ladies were more shy, too, possibly because they were somewhat more

127

'civilised' than the Campas. Neither the Quechua nor the Campa women were in the least embarrassed or selfconscious about feeding their babies in public. Not so the Shipibo. They were obviously far more coy at being seen by men, and covered both themselves and their babies at the breast.

The hovercraft was no sooner repaired and on her way again, hotly pursued by the others, when a crack and a rumbling noise signalled more trouble. We tied up to the bank and floated while we investigated. A fan blade had broken off as it rubbed against the flexible duct.

An hour later Allen and Ricardo had fitted the replacement fan, after filing down the blades to avoid a recurrence. It had been an awkward task, especially when floating on the river. The worst danger was that of dropping the six fan securing bolts into the opaque water. But now we were back on course and there was time to enjoy our surroundings. Just before leaving home many of us had seen the hauntingly beautiful B.B.C. TV film *Flight of the Condor*. I had been disappointed not to see any condors, even as we drove through the high mountain passes, but this was my chance. A pair of the magnificent birds were startled into flight as we passed, showing off their 2½-metres wingspan as they lifted away from their riverside feast.

We saw porpoises too. Few could believe their eyes, but there was no doubt about it. One, two or three gambolled and played in tandem or in parallel in front of us. Fresh-water porpoises, now to be entertaining company for us all the way to Pucallpa.

Later that day we came across a sawmill. On reflection, we were surprised that we had not seen one before; the Amazon is overwhelmingly rich in wood. Here there were piles of logs that dwarfed the man standing beside them. Tree trunks, some of them three metres in diameter, lay in piles by the river. They were enormous. Looking at the surroundings of the factory, we realised that the workmen had had to travel deep into the jungle to get timber, since the river bank sported only a mass of skinny trees.

Galilea was to be our night stop, and a fairly eventful one too! As we approached Galilea, confused because the river didn't seem to be tallying with the map, a storm darkened the sky ahead. Cathy, driving the hovercraft, struggled against a strengthening wind which was whipping up waves in the middle of the wide expanse of water. For the moment we were sheltered by the right bank of the river, but as the Ucayali turned to the right the benefit was lost, and Cathy needed full power to stay above hump speed. The obvious tactic was to stick to one bank or the other. As we suspected that Galilea, on the left bank, would be coming up soon, we crossed the wind-swept river to that side. As soon as we closed with the bank, a strip of calmer water was clearly visible, and as we slipped into the area of lighter wind it marked out, our speed immediately started to pick up. We were passing houses now, and through small gaps in the trees we could see settlements. In front of one of them was a faded signboard: 'Galilea'. This was the place, and the Geminis arrived there almost simultaneously.

Ricardo and I searched for a parking spot. The only possibility was a small gap in the trees with a sloping bank, some 1,200 metres from the main camp. I took a run at it, and parked the craft on the slope with about half of its length out of the water, and the stern part-floating in the shallow water, and part-resting on the river bed. Neither of us relished the idea of sleeping in the craft on such a slope, and decided to find a place in the village.

The settlement had an air of faded elegance. The step up from the riverside signpost which declared 'Principal Port of Galilea. Welcome!' led past a dump of palm tree roofing fronds and on to the football pitch. Directly ahead was the school, a permanent building, with a stout wooden superstructure. It sat in a hollow which seemed to us unusual. Perhaps the river did not reach that far in the high water season? If it did, it would cover the base of the building by about a metre. The school-master offered us the facilities of the school for our overnight stay. To fit us all into the school would have meant removing all of the heavy iron-framed chairs and desks, so most of the team opted for tents.

Ricardo and I laid claim to floor space and went back to remove the padded seats from 06, to soften the hard schoolroom floor. The walk through the cool banana plantations took a

129

quarter of an hour, the trees forming a picturesque avenue, curling gracefully over our heads. The path was wide and well-used, and the river could be seen a few metres away through dangling bunches of green unripened bananas.

Suddenly our peaceful mood was shattered. As we approached the River Rover we found that it had shifted in the forty minutes since we had left it. It had tipped up to a more severe angle, and the water was further up the stern. As we stepped on to the side decks to check the engine compartment, the stern sank further into the soft mud and the craft lurched into an even crazier attitude. Water was pouring through the lift duct into the engine compartment. I started the engine to try for enough air pressure to resist the flow of water, but the water level was now up to the bottom of the thrust fans and one of the blades twisted round to almost 90°, through the force of the water. River Rover 06 was sinking fast.

There was little we could do alone, so Ricardo ran off to get more manpower, while I started shifting heavy items out of the craft. Twenty long minutes later, help finally arrived, even though Ricardo had run all the way. I had been pumping water out of the engine compartment with the manual bilge pump, like Canute pushing back the sea. The water was now up to the oil cooler and seemed set to contaminate the engine. The only hope seemed to be to push the craft off the slope and get it floating level, when there would be plenty of buoyancy. The danger was that we would simply push the stern deeper into the mud. Even so, it had to be tried. We retied the rope I had secured to a banana tree of doubtful strength and then the assembled company pushed the craft off. I sat inside and pumped as if my life depended on it. The stern sank deeper into the water and then, mercifully, lurched up to float horizontally. I kept pumping, but I was now able to make an impression on the six inches of water washing around the base of the engine, and the level steadily fell. I tried the engine and found that it still ran, but the twisted blade was causing vibration and there was no time to change the fan before dusk. A plan was quickly hammered out – the team on shore would pull the craft with ropes on to the bank while I hovered it at as high an r.p.m. as I could muster without severe vibration and possible damage. The local farmer lent a spade to even out the steep slope, and made an unsolicited offer to cut down three banana trees to widen the opening. With grateful thanks, the offer was refused.

'*Dicho y hecho*,' the Peruvians say: 'No sooner said than done.' The bulk of the water was pumped out to reduce weight. The ropes were attached; the throttle opened to 3,000 r.p.m. One strenuous pull, and the craft sat high and dry on the bank. Problem solved. Back to the hexamine stoves, and the commandeered schoolroom.

'Adventure creeps up on you,' Mike said as we walked back, 'when you least expect it.'

CHAPTER TEN

The Home Straight

THE FINAL DAY opened in optimism. We had travelled over eight hundred accident-free kilometres, barring a minor sinking, and even there disaster had been averted just in time. The distance to our final goal, Pucallpa, was only 130 kilometres, barely half a day's journey. True, we had only the vaguest idea of what would meet us, or how we would get to the Wycliffe Bible Translators at Yarinacocha, where 06 was to be housed. But no matter. Most were anxious simply to arrive.

Today was also the leader's day. Mike had graciously delegated the planning and control of the journey to me, himself taking a background position in the events he had brought about by his dogged tenacity. But he was to drive the craft the last miles into Pucallpa.

The general eagerness to reach the end of the journey overshadowed any regrets we may have had to leave Galilea. Yet it had probably been our best night stop. Dick Bell had befriended a family; the eldest girl, Liliana, was fourteen; the next, Jenefe, was eight the day we left; and the boy was six. The mild and affectionate children had watched with Dick and the others the amazing swarm of dragonflies that had appeared just before sunset. They were large ones, double winged, with blue torsos. Hundreds of them, whirring and dodging about, noses into the wind. They had come from nowhere, stayed to entertain us with an impromptu floor show, and disappeared again without trace. The Spanish name for dragonfly is *la libelula*. The Cocama called it *chinchileja*. Dick wondered if every language in the world used such unusual and attractive names for this delightful insect.

The Galilea schoolroom had been the scene for a torchlit game of Uckers, the grown-up Service equivalent of Ludo. The engineers had made the Uckers board, counters and dice in some spare moments in the workshop in San Francisco. And, of course, it had to be brought down with us on the canoe. If we could bring the kitchen sink, we had to have the Uckers. And Galilea had been a gentle reintroduction to a more civilized lifestyle. There was a hole in the ground in a hut near the school that was the closest we had seen to a real toilet for some days!

The dawn was startlingly red, glowing shafts of fire shooting up through the timid clouds like a warrior thirsting for adventure. Alas, the tropical sun rises and sets too quickly, and only those out strolling or praying or meditating in the early morning saw the best of it.

Before we set off, Dick was taken by the family to their house. Raised on stilts, it had tightly fitted floor-boards throughout, made of stout Amazonian hardwood. The little steps from the ground led to an open balustraded space, which served as a verandah, dining room (in one corner), and playspace for the children. Open plan homes are very sensible in the tropics. On the right of the verandah was the bedroom. The whole family slept in the one room, but all had individual beds. The bases of the beds were solid, but they had thin mattresses, bottom sheets, and a thicker blanket for the covering, rather on the lines of a thin duvet, as well as mosquito nets. To the left of the verandah was another room, in which a relative was living. Both rooms were well built of solid planked wood, completely draught free, and had a ceiling and gauze-covered windows. From the near left-hand side of the verandah, steps led down to the kitchen, which would presumably be flooded out in the rainy season. The cooking was done on a wood fire between a pair of logs, and the soot-blackened utensils were stored on rudimentary shelves, with a few days' groceries. The supplies were neither abundant nor frugal. Outside, at the back, was a little pen in which two pigs were sniffing and snorting, and chickens, scratching around in the dust which surrounded the house, completed the family.

133

The Geminis were ready. In keeping with the 'end of term' atmosphere, the threadbare cord trousers I had used for the journey were consigned to the bonfire. Both Geminis sped along together, often inches apart, with Jim bashing Tony about the head with his hat! We thought there would be just enough fuel to reach Pucallpa, but wanted to have some in reserve, so we were looking out for a refuelling stop. Shortly after Masisea a collection of buildings appeared on the left bank, with a brightly-coloured flower garden, and fuel drums under a shelter.

The place was more sophisticated than we had expected: a tree-shaded seat and cold drinks out of the giant fridge. Abba (in Spanish) from a cassette recorder. A green parrot sitting on the shoulder of the tall auburn-haired woman who served the Coca-Cola.

The short stop turned into a longer one when we discovered that the port aft tube on Tony's Gemini was deflating – a gash had suddenly appeared in the sturdy rubber. Tony and Stuart found adhesive and material, and set about applying a patch, and while it dried we tried to photograph the freshwater dolphins as they jumped in pairs from the calm river surface. Brian Holdsworth succumbed to the sultry atmosphere and took a dignified nap.

The whole stop lasted about one and a half hours, and destroyed the lead the advance party had on the others. Once we got under way again, the patch started to tear off with the force of the water moving over it. Within twenty minutes it was all but gone. Tony produced a metal patch of the type which is inserted in the hole and then is screwed down on to the material from both sides. It held, after a fashion, but we left the foot pump attached and I kept pumping air into the tube, at a slow, steady rate, to replace any losses.

We turned into a narrow channel which we hoped was the final stretch. We were doubtful for a few minutes, but then started to see boats going the other way. They had to be coming from somewhere. Sure enough, a little before two p.m., industrial buildings started to come into view. 'Twelve o'clock, one mile!' I shouted to Tony over the roar of the Johnson outboard. 'That's Pucallpa.' He grinned with a flush of pride. His boats had made it.

As we drew closer we could pick out more detail of the city. It seemed incongruous after our days of deserted stretches of river and remote villages. Dilapidated riverside shacks faced rows of boats of every size and type, unloading goods which they had brought up the Amazon. Once the inflatables were tied up at a ladder on the modern-looking pontoon pier, Ricardo, James and I went off to try and contact Yarinacocha to say 'Here we are.' Not a hope. We found ourselves being questioned by security guards as to why we were inside the fenced area of the dock. We explained ourselves to one official after another – they would not let us unload without official permission. After some persuasion they let us phone Yarinacocha. No reply.

Meanwhile the hovercraft arrived, chased in by a police 'speed' boat! When Mike wanted to reposition the triumphant River Rover to allow Stu to film the historic arrival (a heavy-breathing policeman's hand had covered the camera at the first attempt), the police threatened arrest if he moved the craft. He did, but it was not Mike they arrested. Tony and I were taken immediately to the Port Police Authority, under guard, to explain ourselves.

In other circumstances we would have enjoyed the crazy hilarity of our trip to the police station. We were bundled into the severely underpowered little aluminium boat, the bows pointing crazily into the air in protest at our extra weight. Twice we had to stop to disentangle a mass of weeds from the propeller and it seemed that there was severe danger of Tony's expertise with outboards being needed. My greatest worry, though, was that Tony, who obviously does not take kindly to incarceration, would allow his seething temper to surface.

As we sat in the *Capitanía*'s dingy corridor, wondering how we could minimise the sentence for illegal import of hovercraft through a free port without documentation, Tony reached into his wallet and unfolded a scrap of paper.

'Would this help?' he asked. 'I thought it might be useful, so I kept it.' He had in his hand a photocopy of a letter, signed by the Private Secretary of the *Presidente de la Republica*, extolling the virtues of our project. The letter was passed from hand to hand. Someone rushed off to find the Peruvian government

135

equivalent of *Who's Who*, to check that the person named on the letter really was who we said he was. And, eventually, all concerned decided that this was an Important Case, and we were summoned to see the *Capitan*. I explained who we were and showed him on the map where we had come from, dropping the word *Presidente* at least twice in every sentence. '*Bueno*,' said the swarthy *Capitan* at last, 'You can go.'

A policeman was detailed to take us through the weed-infested harbour back to the boats. The canoe had arrived and Mike sent the doctors, girls, Dick Bell and James off to Yarinacocha by taxi, to try to make contact in person. Ricardo and I went to try the phone again, and to visit the shipping agents' office to get permission to offload, but we received no sympathy.

'You need authorisation from the *Capitanía* first,' they explained. We went back to find that the boats had already been unloaded on to the pier!

As it turned out, the offloading was not such a good move. Yarinacocha was accessible by river! Stewart Mackintosh and Tito Paredes, our contacts with the recipients of 06, had arrived, and with them a local boatman, Bernadino, who knew the way to Yarinacocha – it would take one and a half hours, and we would not need to lift the River Rover on to a truck. The weary team began to reload the boats.

The taxi party missed this particular entertainment. They had carried their rucksacks through the main gate, and stopped at a cafe for a *gaseosa*, a soft drink, before seeking out some taxis. The weather was close, tropical and stifling, and even the half-kilometre walk was sufficient to drench them with perspiration and fatigue. Taxis were unearthed, the price agreed on – very important – and they piled in, only to pile out again as one taxi went axle deep into an unmarked hole in the concrete. The weary travellers had to lift it out, before driving on through Pucallpa.

It was a novelty to travel on metalled roads, the first since Ayacucho, but on the outskirts of the city the normal earth road continued. The wooden houses alongside were covered to waist height with red dust. None of the houses was fenced; attitudes to real estate are different when there is plenty of space. It was typical of a tropical township, with shops selling everything, interspersed with small factories, mostly dealing in wood. There was even a Bingo Club. The road took them past the Electriciy Power Station, and out into the countryside, as the ugly turkey-buzzards which populated the town rubbish tip looked on.

The entrance to the Wycliffe H.Q. compound was a gate with the S.I.L. credentials alongside it, written in Spanish. The Summer Institute of Linguistics is the secular name for the Wycliffe Bible Translators, and the two names are almost interchangeable. In Spanish, 'S.I.L.' translates to 'I.L.V.' – *Instituto Linguistico de Verano*.

It was a different world inside. Beautifully built houses, set in their own grounds, lined the road. Each house was unique, individually designed, and each had its garden with a well-cut lawn overshadowed by an array of exotic trees. Scent filled the air, and the whole area was fragrant with serenity, peace and prosperity. The Americans, even more than the British, take their homes and comforts abroad with them. For missionaries, the price is high, and many years of hard sweat were needed to bring this place up to this attractive standard. The site now held two hundred families. We later learned that the first five houses had been built of mahogany. The Americans were the only ones in the area at that time who appreciated the value of good wood and it was abundantly available. The Peruvians soon caught up with them.

The little taxi party bustled around, looking for someone important. Eventually a man called Bruce turned up; he was the man in charge of the radio links with the missionaries out in the *selva*, and a real administrator. Quiet, confident, unflusterable, gently efficient, he showed them to a place on the airfield by the windsock, overlooking the lake, where the tents could be pitched. In the neat, efficient aircraft hangar, drinking water was available. From a *tap*! Incredible! After more than two months of fighting for every drop of *agua potable*, they were offered limitless drinking water from a tap. Open-mouthed, they looked at the water dripping into a bisected 50-gallon drum, where the aviation engineers washed their hands. The British visitors drank the sweet, cool water. Only at moments

137

like this could one appreciate just how much of our lives over the last few months had been spent in just getting drinking water. Chris and Tim at San Francisco went every other day to fill up the 250-gallon water tank. Here it was free. Maybe we will never again forget the cost of having clean water; perhaps we will remember those in the Third World whose whole lives would be spent on fetching water to live.

Bruce mentioned that the lake was excellent for swimming. 'There are quite a few piranha fish,' he said, 'but they won't molest you. But don't swim after five thirty p.m. as the sting-rays come to the shallows then, and they will go for you.'

None of the party had washed properly in five days. As soon as they had put up their tents, they dived into the 80°F water. Utter bliss. What a luxury to be clean.

The little group prepared for the arrival of the rest of us as best they could, and awaited our appearance. The sun went down in an extravaganza of glorious yellow, and still we had not turned up. An uncomfortable feeling spread through them that all was not well. Dick started to feel he should be praying about our safety. But then James arrived. He had returned to the dock, and had seen us board the boats. We would soon be arriving. There was no problem.

John Bush, the senior aircraft engineer, came out to invite them to sleep in the Ops Centre overnight. Rain was threatening. They gladly accepted, and slept soundly all night, on comfortable cushions in a cosy room, glad to be back in civilization.

Their relief on our behalf was premature, and Dick's inner prompting had been correct. At this last stage we had come across one of the most frustrating difficulties of the whole expedition.

After the 'practice unload and load' drill under the relentless sun, the spirits of the main party could not have been described as high. Journey's end at Pucallpa was not turning out quite as we had expected. Before we could start the one and a half hour journey to Yarinacocha, we had to collect two drums of fuel in Pucallpa for the week of hovercraft training we were to give to the church people. Until this afternoon, we had not even known that such a week was planned. As befits a river city, the fuel was to be collected from a ship.

The *Princesa de la Urubamba* was used by a group of Machiguenga Indians with whom a Wycliffe couple had worked for twenty-five years. At the moment it was moored at Pucallpa, and our little flotilla caused quite a stir as we tied up alongside to refuel. The *Princesa* even seemed to take on a list with the weight of onlookers on the side nearest us. The deck was a scene of utter confusion. In Peru, Parkinson's Law has to be modified slightly; work expands to fill *twice* the time available to complete it. We were eating into the remaining daylight, and we had not even left Pucallpa.

At last the little fleet was ready to leave port. Our new-found guide, Bernadino, would lead the way in one of the Geminis; the canoe would follow the two inflatables, and the hovercraft would take up the rear. It was the only way to keep the dissimilar craft together, a task I had decided not even to try on the long journey to Pucallpa. We moved down the broad Ucayali river, the hovercraft weaving to and fro as Mike tried to match the canoe's stately progress.

The river seemed to go on for ever. People glanced nervously at their watches. Nearly an hour passed before Bernadino finally settled on a narrow inlet to the left. Lake Yarinacocha is a long narrow oxbow parallel to the Ucayali, which was formed – who knows when – as the river changed its course. The lake is connected to the mighty river at each end by a channel or *caño*, but only the one at the northern end was passable. We knew that, because Bernadino had been along it only six days previously.

We turned into the 25-metre-wide channel, but 500 metres further on, Bernadino directed us into an even narrower channel on the right where we were confronted with a gloomy sight. A log-jam. Mike parked the River Rover on a steep bank near a village and we walked to a vantage point to look at the mass of floating timber. There was no way that the craft could hover over the mass of twisted branches that floated on the water. But the boats had a chance.

'Right,' I decided. 'We'll secure the hovercraft here, and collect it tomorrow. The other three boats will go on.' Although it would be dark by the time we reached the lake, the lights of the Wycliffe Settlement would be visible across the open water. We piled aboard the boats, ready for battle with the logs!

By now we were a somewhat lame army. Every member was weary from the day's journey and the confused changes of plan in the jungle heat of Pucallpa. Tony's Gemini was holed, a leaky stopper sealing a flaccid tube; and a bent throttle linkage made the engine difficult to control. Even Mike was now unable to produce spares. The rigid-hulled canoe seemed the best bet to part the logs and clear a path, although its great length would be unmanoeuvrable on the sharp bends. The second Gemini, captained by Stuart Forbes, was perhaps in the best situation. Its hull was undamaged and it was equipped with an expensive steel propeller which would cut like a knife through the less substantial wood. Tony's brittle aluminium propeller was liable to shatter at any moment on the underwater obstructions.

As we ploughed through the lattice of dead timber, it soon became apparent that we could not simply power our way through the obstructions. Logs lay in every direction and extended from the surface down to an unknown depth. Tree trunks and branches intertwined in a confused mass. Some had to be dragged aside; some had to be pushed down into the water; some had to be chopped away with knives and machetes. We had thought that the canoe could clear a path, but it was not that easy. As soon as a gap was opened, it closed up again as the logs drifted in behind the boats. Later we learned more about the way the flow through the *caño* changed. When the river was falling, the lake tended to empty into the river, flushing out the *caños*, as the water flowed out towards the Ucayali. But when the river was rising, it was a different story. The river would try to fill up the lake and, of course, as we had seen, along with the floodwaters came the timber debris. The current into the lake was strong, and on bends the logs would be forced by the current to pile up, like rush-hour passengers on the London Underground as they reach the ticket barrier.

Every metre of progress had to be fought for. Logs were pushed aside with paddles, boots, anything that could be used. The crews worked almost in silence. Only occasionally was the stillness broken by grunts and groans, as a strenuous

140

heave shifted the recalcitrant timber. Arms stretched down to shoulder depth into the dank water under the Geminis, to clear debris away from the propellers.

It began to get dark. We had been too busy to worry about torches, but now we rummaged for them in our packs.

'We've got into clear water!' The exultant cry came from the canoe ahead, followed almost immediately by a groan.

'Oh no! There's another jam.'

The short straight section was clear, but the next bend was blocked by yet another mesh of timber.

The overhanging jungle canopy excluded any moonlight there might have been. The sensation was as disconcerting as if we were in a darkened tunnel. Doug hooked the powerful Lucas searchlight up to the generator, and Mike took it upon himself to direct the light. The penetrating beam waved to and fro, lighting up the river and showing a depressing stretch of logs ahead. Hordes of insects swarmed towards the light source, forcing Mike to cover himself and the lamp in mosquito nets. Those who were not engaged in forcing the canoe through the logs retreated to bow and stern, leaving our leader sitting in splendid isolation amidships, surrounded by a cloud of voracious insects.

The sudden bonus of light added some logic to the weary clearance of rotten branches, but tempers were becoming frayed. By now the Gemini crews were spending less time inside the boats than outside. The technique was simple. Just hold on to the boat, step on an apparently solid log, and hope. The log would sink, of course, but as it met with resistance from sticks and boughs criss-crossed beneath it, the downward progress would become slower. Eventually, one hoped, at about thigh-depth, one would have a firm foothold. It did not always work; Brian Holdsworth sank to a depth of about seven feet without finding a foothold – and he is only 5 feet 8 inches tall! Once we had a place for at least one foot, we would lift the boat over the more stubborn floating trees, while the coxswain gunned the engine. It was not very long before our three-bladed propeller had become a two-bladed one.

Another clear stretch confirmed our suspicions about the strength of the current. We overtook a complete tree which was floating at about six knots. Ahead lay an area of standing trees through which the water flowed and as we ducked their over-hanging boughs, we heard a voice from the inky blackness ahead.

'Watch out for that branch, I saw a tree snake on it.'

Brian, whose hand was just holding the said branch to one side, dropped to the rubber floor of the boat. An evil chuckle emanated from the other inflatable: the age of humour is not dead.

Midnight approached. Aching and mosquito-bitten, the ex-hausted team worked on but there was no telling how many more blockages lay ahead. When an abandoned village came into sight with enough space to camp, the decision was immediate.

With relief, we called a halt. Tents were put up in record time and sleep came quickly. By five in the morning, Mike and Tony had walked along the bank for a 'recce'. After the next log-jam, they reported, there was clear water as far as they could see.

The next morning, with renewed enthusiasm, we pressed on, having discovered that only one more log-jam separated us and the lake. In daylight, the task was easier. Vast spiders' webs hung over the water, and 50 metres ahead, a dolphin broke the glassy surface. And round the next corner we feasted our eyes on the lake.

What a sight! It was a mile wide, and the far end was out of view. The water itself was the colour of thin Green Pea soup and the temperature about 80°F. An irresistible temptation. The Geminis stopped in the centre of the lake while their crews plunged over the side to bathe in the tropical waters.

At the S.I.L. headquarters, the well-rested advance party awaited us.

'What kept you?' called the clean, neatly-dressed Stu Antrobus. British explorers have reserves of energy that even they do not know about. Suddenly four of the bedraggled new arrivals grabbed a limb each, and Stu found himself swimming in the lake – neat clothes and all.

CHAPTER ELEVEN

Jungletown U.S.A.

As THE SKY above the lakeside Mission blackened, our rate of unloading suddenly accelerated. We completed it just in time, before we were attacked by one of those tropical downpours that leave one speechless. We sheltered inside the hangar, and discovered the halved oil drum with a tap above it. I myself stripped down to swimming trunks, threw five days' clothes into a big plastic sack, and searched out my wash kit. For rinsing, the tap was superfluous. Later, someone handed me a Polaroid photo of myself, standing under the overflowing gutter, rinsing out soap and shampoo. We couldn't speak without shouting. The rain hammered onto the corrugated iron roof, killing any conversation, but we did not mind. Most of us were glad just to recuperate.

Meanwhile, those who had stayed the night had been exploring. They had all been invited to Wayne and Betty Snell's for breakfast, sampling home-made jam, waffles and honey, and *Yerba Luisa* tea; 'Louise's Grass', by translation. Appropriate, since the Snells had offered Louise and Cathy their spare room. Horace and Cathy visited the medical post, and talked to the hard-worked nurse there. There had not been a doctor for a while, and our medical and dental team agreed to spend some time helping in the clinic. Dick Bell discovered the Print Shop. Cathy and James searched out the Launderama, took note of the board which said, 'Do not put shoes in the washing machines', and put the team's name down for ten thirty a.m. The booking later expanded to include most of the day. I confirmed the Americans' fears about the crazy British, by walking around in the pouring rain in my swimming trunks, with my only clean and dry set of clothes wrapped in polythene under my arm.

The people of this little Christian township refused to accept that we did not want to bother them. Hospitality was offered to everyone; members of the team lived among the different nations, in the different houses, sleeping on a variety of beds; and loved it. Although most of the team were the rugged sort, enjoying the challenge of adventure in the wilds, all enjoyed being fussed over, appreciating the unaccustomed luxury. Everything at Yarinacocha was a pleasure. The lay-out, the people, the homes, the generosity, the electricity, the drinking water, the shops, the maintenance, the trees and flowers, the church services and prayer meetings – it seemed to us like Heaven on Earth.

Most interesting to us Servicemen was the hangar. J.A.A.R.S. (the Jungle Aviation and Radio Service) is the air arm of the S.I.L., with its Headquarters at Yarinacocha, and is headed by Leo Lance. He is a dynamic extrovert, carefully modified by years of Christian discipline to be gracious, humble, unflustered and wise. We had great respect both for him and for his wife, Ann, who rose at four a.m. most mornings to cook tons of breakfast for us. Leo's chief engineer is John Bush, efficient, precise, helpful, intense, round and jolly. The team watched this hive of engineering industry very carefully. Not everyone in the team had always been impressed with the activities of Christians, but this place tended to silence the critics. It was our kind of engineering. No corners were cut; no rules were bent. So good was it that the Peruvian Air Force sent aircraft there for their routine servicing; it was of a higher standard than their own.

Mike arranged for Stu Antrobus's release home. Stu had left a wife with two young toddlers back in Plymouth, and needed to get back to them. He took the Aeroperu flight out that night: we were sorry to lose him.

Leo gave us all breakfast on Sunday morning. At ten o'clock some of us went to morning Bible Study, which was held for all ages, while others challenged the young people in the compound to volleyball – and lost. The whole team went to

James McClune opens the village water supply

First taste of clean, running water

Log jam

Journey's end

A world record for Jim Mudie

Below: Julian Latham

Presidential Palace,
Lima

Handover

the morning service, where Mike introduced us, and said something about the Expedition. There were over three hundred people in the service, and they welcomed us warmly.

We were left with the problem of how to get the hovercraft to Yarinacocha, and how to get the canoe back to Pucallpa, and on its way to San Francisco. Somehow, it had to get through one of the *caños* and tackle the log-jams again. It was a daunting thought.

We had come in through the northern *caño*. Now we would see what the southern one was like. We set out in the beautiful Sunday afternoon sunshine through the water hyacinth which congested the southern end of the lake, gambolling porpoises keeping us company. It felt like a Sunday afternoon outing.

We missed the *caño* entrance, and had to retrace our steps. When we found it, it was carpeted with lily-pads and watercress. Our passage disturbed a number of Lily-trotters, birds with huge toes with which to walk on the water-lilies. In our company were some of the strong young American Christians, who were game for any challenge. They came complete with axes, saws, and 'levers – various'. The *caño* was narrow, a few metres to start with, but it soon shrivelled to become almost impossible to negotiate. One or two trees had fallen by the edges, and the 17-metre canoe had trouble weaving round them in the narrow confines. Overhanging branches, festooned with wasps' nests and vicious thorns, so covered our route that we had to crouch down in the canoe while it crept laboriously under the entanglements. We struggled along the *caño* sometimes having to cut down branches that completely blocked our way.

A few yards further into the entangled greenery, the *caño* widened slightly, and we saw a *peci-peci* tied up at the bank. A path led to a little homestead, where a fisherman was sitting. We asked him if the *caño* was open further up.

'No,' he said, 'there are two trees blocking it.' As we moved on to investigate, the man followed us in a small canoe.

At three thirty p.m. we arrived at the trees. The second tree looked quite rotten and would be easy to deal with. But to do that we had to get past the first one. The huge trunk lay right across the channel, its base partly in the water. It was nearly four feet in diameter. We couldn't go underneath or around it.

145

We needed more equipment – a chainsaw, a block and tackle, and more time than we had this afternoon. A quick 'recce' along the bank showed that there were few problems beyond this point, but it also showed that these trees had not fallen across the *caño*. They had been felled. The channel had been blocked deliberately. But why? Filing away the intriguing query, we decided to retreat, and return on Monday with more equipment.

Putting the Johnson into reverse nearly capsized the fisherman, who had been watching the proceedings in silence. We shrugged our shoulders and told him it was too difficult a task to complete in the time, asking him who had cut the trees. 'I did,' he confessed. During the high season, many fishermen from the Rio came through the *caño* to fish in the lake – a better prospect than their own territory. He had grown tired of that, so, to protect his fishing rights, he had blocked the *caño* for everybody. A selfish action, with repercussions beyond his intentions.

The hardest task on the return journey was trying to turn the canoe round in the *caño*. Even at the widest place, it took three-quarters of an hour of levering, straining, yanking, shoving, punting, pushing, pulling, heaving, and generally wishing we hadn't started. We arrived back at S.I.L. as dusk was falling, abandoning the southern *caño* for another day.

Anne and Leo Lance had invited the whole team to supper, and the plans for the coming days were hammered out in their open-plan living room. Most of the Team were going away on individual expeditions around Peru, and four were staying in Yarinacocha. They were Mike, James, Roy and Dick Bell. Leo was asked if they could borrow a J.A.A.R.S. Helio aircraft to recover the hovercraft. To fit into their busy schedule, it would only be available at seven thirty a.m., for no more than an hour. And Leo would come too.

Mike and Dick were down at the Ops Centre at six fifteen a.m. James was to stand by for a radio call before trying to get the canoe out. He was to rustle up his own crew. Roy was to investigate whether the Yarinacocha lorry would carry the hovercraft and take it, with Wayne, to the docks.

The Helio took off at seven thirty a.m. with Leo in the hot

seat, and Steve, a young pilot who was just settling in at the base, in the other. They looked at the *caños*, the southern one first. It was clear up to the two trees of yesterday, and they could even see the swathe cut into the watercress by the canoe. They traced the *caño* to see if it was clear to the Rio Ucayali. After some metres, it turned right, and opened up. There were no other blockages that they could see. It wove its meandering course for another kilometre, and ended up in a lake which was cut off from the main river by a bank. Had we managed to struggle through the *caño* on the previous day, we could never have got the canoe out into the open – unless, of course, we had been prepared to empty it and carry it over a two-foot bank first. Time after time during the expedition, we had been blocked, either literally or figuratively. Those of us who believed in the power of prayer had often spent hours or days in puzzlement. But so often the reason had later become clear; this was one such case.

The airborne 'recce' party checked the northern *caño*. The rise in water level, even since Friday night, had dislodged some of the log-jams. There were still about five to negotiate, but it seemed from the air that they were feasible. They flew low over the whole *caño*: the worst log-jam was at the mouth; it was now about 50 metres long. Leo radioed back to Ops Centre with the information and the super-professional engineers 'patched' him through to the dining-room where we were breakfasting.

'Southern *caño* – bad news. Northern *caño* possible, but *palisadas* still there. Take full equipment, and leave as early as possible if you feel it is right to try it.'

James needed no second bidding. He had drummed up volunteers. In fact, he had trouble keeping volunteers away, and many high-school kids, yearning to be in on everything that involved muscle, had to be sadly turned away and sent back to school.

In the Helio Leo looked for a landing spot, close to where the River Rover still stood. Flying low over the *caño* he spotted a stretch of water that was clear of logs and debris. He wound up the pitch, wound down the flaps, and aimed the Helio at this tiny stretch of water. Dick, a pilot of many hours flying experience, was doubtful if it would make it, but thrilled to see an aircraft being worked to its limits. The Helio floats knifed the calm surface at 30 knots and came to rest in a staggeringly short distance. Leo had deliberately stopped near a village, as he had spotted a couple of *peci-pecis* from which they might be able to get a lift. Slowly he turned the Helio in towards the narrow gap in the reeds, cutting the engine before getting too close, and allowing the plane to drift in to the shore. Leo, Mike and Dick jumped ashore with two cans of petrol and the rest of their emergency kit. Steve started the engine and blasted out of the river as swiftly as they had dropped in.

They asked if they could borrow a *peci-peci*, but every owner was away. They walked up the path, lugging the heavy jerrycans. Stops were frequent until they came across a man who agreed to take them in his *peci-peci*, in return for some petrol. It was now only eight a.m. but it felt like midday. He and his son emptied the *peci-peci* of some fruit that looked like cherries, heaved the motor on to its spike at the back of the boat, and they clambered aboard. Leo pointed out a rock that the man had rested the engine on; it was valuable. There were no rocks in Pucallpa. Astonished, Mike and Dick looked around, being familiar with far too many up-river. The ground was mud and reddish clay; and, indeed, there were no stones to be seen anywhere.

It was a lot further than they had thought. Distances are so deceptive from the air. They rounded a bend in the *caño* and saw the hovercraft parked where we had left it, tilted at an alarming angle, looking forlorn and incongruous, and the way to it completely jammed by a *palisada* of logs.

Once the battle through to the hovercraft had been won, an alarming discovery was made: one of the side windows was pushed out. What was missing from inside? The party scrambled up the side. The rope that had held it to the nearest tree was missing, so was a leather chamois. But, amazingly, all else was there. There were expensive H.F. and hand-held radios inside; jerrycans, and all sorts of tools and other equipment.

'Where is the rope?' they asked a villager standing nearby.

'How do I know?' he shrugged. 'You never asked me to guard the boat for you, so I cannot guarantee its safety.' The implication was clear. Pay to have it guarded, or have things taken. Either way, the *gringo* pays.

They got the hovercraft ship-shape, and then talked through a plan of action. Overland routes were investigated, but eventually all agreed that it had to be *palisada* or nothing. They decided to try and take the hovercraft from the grassy bank on which it sat, up the little channel in the logs cut by the *peci-peci* when it had come in. It was on the same side as the hovercraft now was, but it was obstructed by a dozen or so shrubs, some up to two metres high, logs, and a tree full of wasps that had attacked Mike on the way in.

Dick, as the most experienced driver there, got in. Mike sat on the nose to give balance and to push away logs and other obstacles. Leo went in the *peci-peci* to try and open up a channel again, as the hovercraft came slowly behind, always in danger of shredding its skirt on the *peci-peci*'s propeller.

Mike, of course, was attacked by the wasps again, and stuck his head between his knees. The rest of the wasps were blown through thrust fans, which must have surprised them somewhat, and shredded a few. The rest of the escape from the *palisada* was a combination of heaving, pushing, driving, gentle persuading, tree climbing and hard graft. Eventually they reached open water, thanked the *peci-peci* owner profusely, and roared off towards the Ucayali.

Meanwhile Steve had taken the Helio back to Yarinacocha. He planned his sortie to the missionary outpost and overflew the *caño* just after take-off. The hovercraft had left. A radio call was all that was needed to get James away in the canoe with Maxi and Horacio. Bernadino was there with a chain saw. Carlos Pinto, one of the Peruvians Dick was to teach to drive the hovercraft, was included. So was Dan. Dan was a single man whose missionary calling was to go up into the jungle and teach Indian tribes the value of forming their communities into villages. A quiet and gentle man, he had suffered immense deprivation to achieve any success over many years of effort. He had come to Yarinacocha for a short break and to pick up supplies. Now, here he was volunteering for this little expedition.

149

So the canoe was well equipped to battle through the *caño* and succeeded without too much difficulty. The hovercraft had motored down a few hours earlier, and was skimming sweetly over the water when a sudden explosion at the back end, followed by vibration, shocked them into action.

'To the edge!' Dick barked shortly. 'It's a fan-blade gone.' There was no way of telling what other damage might have been done by flying fan-blades. Leo was swift to respond. He turned the craft sharply towards the shore, cutting the motor as they reached the edge. Mike leaped out with a rope that had been hidden in the back, and tied the nose of the hovercraft to a handy tree. As if by magic, five Peruvians appeared to stare. Sure enough, the port fan was broken, two of the blades were gone. Six self-locking nuts held the fan on. Leo wielded a spanner at the front end, and Dick did the same behind the fan. It was awkward, as the craft kept moving its rump out into the Rio, and there was nowhere else to stand except in the water. Finally it was done, and the rest of the journey to Pucallpa was without incident.

They landed at the same place in the over-populated dock that Mike had found when he initially arrived at Pucallpa – a muddy slope mined with broken bottles and discarded tin cans.

They expected Wayne and Roy to be there, perhaps with the lorry from Yarinacocha on which to transport the hovercraft to the lake. They waited half an hour. Mike decided to go and search for them, vanishing with Leo into the dockside confusion. Dick guarded the hovercraft, as always finding a little crowd to talk to.

After another hour or so, Wayne and Roy appeared. Of course, they hadn't seen Mike or Leo. Roy had measured the compound lorry, but found it too small for the hovercraft. He guarded the hovercraft while Wayne and Dick walked up to the dock to see if they could get hold of a lorry that could do the job. They found one that would be available for hire at a price they negotiated down to a mildly extortionate level. It would be ready at any moment.

'Any moment' turned out to be two hours later, but while they waited they saw the red and blue lines of *Juliancito*, the canoe, growl into port. The two major prayers of the day had been answered.

Even when they had the truck, there were the normal minor problems of bureaucracy and paperwork and pock-marked roads to deal with, but eventually the seven-mile trip to Yarinacocha was completed. A group of teenagers playing volleyball in the compound stopped and burst spontaneously into applause. The bizarre problems of this unusual project had caught the imagination of the missionary township.

The same day, Horace and David helped in the compound clinic. They had been asked to attend to a number of missionaries with outstanding medical problems. There had not been a doctor around for a long time, and it was urgent that a professional opinion be sought for some of them.

In the morning they took a clinic for the Indian people. Mike Harvey, the Pharmacist and Administrator, the senior nursing sister, Ruth, and four qualified nurses all attended. They treated cases of worms, chest infections, vaginal infections, urethritis and pulmonary fibrosis, and did ante-natal care. David was even asked to go to the farm and treat a calf with a broken leg. The clinic at Yarinacocha teaches, services and supplies over fifty Health Promoters in the jungle. In the clinic that morning some of the girls were busy packing drugs for an annual flight for one Promoter. Some of the Promoters only come to the S.I.L. once a year, when they stock up with a whole year's medicines.

After the morning clinic, David and Horace were taken round the S.I.L. museum and Translation Centre. There they played with a seven-foot-long blowpipe, and curare-tipped poisonous darts, used by some of the northern tribes.

'I have seen an Indian put three darts within an inch of each other at 100 feet,' said Floyd Lyon, their guide. 'There are fifty-one separate languages in Peru, and S.I.L. are working on thirty at present. We have been here for thirty-five years, and have completed New Testaments in sixteen of the languages.' Normal translation of the New Testament takes twenty-five years, but the acquisition of computer word processors has revolutionised their system, and reduced the time to ten to

151

twelve years. David took a photograph of Indian message drums and a word processor, fascinated by the contrast in methods of communication.

S.I.L. also write down and publish folk-lore and tribal tales, believing these to be important in maintaining the tribe's heritage. Unlike many of the anthropologists who criticise their work, they spend years, even decades, learning the customs and traditions of the tribe, as well as its language. They are better placed than most to appreciate how misleading the word 'primitive' can be. The Indians' intelligence, often extremely high, is manifested in ways which are alien to us.

In the Machiguenga tribe where Wayne and Betty Snell had spent most of their lives, a Chief Orator is appointed to instruct the tribe. If a member wished to challenge him for the position, he has to listen to the Orator speaking through a whole night – twelve long hours – and then repeat all that he said, word for word, on the following night. If he gets it right, he gets the job. One Moisha boy, aged eleven, was able to name and identify 336 out of 470 known species of birds in the area.

At two p.m. it was the missionaries' turn to take advantage of the skill of the visiting doctors. They dealt with the usual variety of problems found in general practice: skin rashes, chronic fungal ear infections, hypostatic oedema from varicose veins, etc. But just as they were leaving, a little seven-year-old Indian boy was brought in with a fracture of the tibia and fibula of his left leg. He had a history of several previous fractures and David was amazed to notice the bright blue tinge of the whites of his eyes, a classic sign. Here, tucked away in the jungle, was this remarkably rare condition that every medical student learns about – Fragilitas Ossium. They set his bones, using valium to calm him down, having taken an X-ray on the spot. Everything in the clinic was very modern, enabling the doctors to give complete therapy and thus aid rapid recovery. Having set the bones, they applied Plaster of Paris, and immediately the boy began to feel more comfortable.

'I wish all those thousands of pounds' worth of drugs we had to leave at San Francisco, never to be used, could have been brought here,' wrote David later. 'They would have been put to full and proper use right away. Mike Harvey experiences a chronic shortage of drugs, many orders never getting through, and Customs delaying some for up to nine months. Nevertheless, S.I.L. enjoys the best possible relationship with the current Peruvian Government. The more I see of this Mission Station, the more profoundly impressed I am. I can honestly say that I have never seen or ever heard of such a superb Christian venture, from all points of view, spiritual through to practical, as I see everywhere here.'

Tuesday morning saw the start of a hectic training programme. Even though Mike, Roy, James and Dick wondered now and again what excitements lay before their companions on the tourist trails, each felt delighted and privileged to remain at S.I.L. and take part in this work.

Dick had seven students, each vitally important in his or her own right.

Leo Lance, the head of J.A.A.R.S. was to become the chief hovercraft instructor when Dick left.

Dr. Stewart Mackintosh was the Regions Beyond Missionary Union representative, who had come out to Pucallpa to feed the hovercraft through into regular use.

Tito Paredes, a Peruvian born in Huancayo, was leader of C.E.M.A.A., the main evangelical church in Peru. He was a Doctor of Anthropology from the University of California in Los Angeles, and a Master of Divinity from Fuller Theological Seminary. He was at present teaching in Lima Theological Seminary. A very important man, but he was also kind, humble, enthusiastic and companionable.

Angel Diaz was a member of the Machiguenga tribe. He was a young man of about twenty-five, but had already become one of three leaders of the Machiguenga Christian Church. He was pastor to a number of churches up the Urubamba, and was active as a Bible teacher and lecturer in schools and colleges. He was a shy man, quiet and gentle. But the outward appearance was deceptive; he hid a tenacity, and power, and intelligence that justified all that was spoken of him.

Carlos Pinto was a first-year university student in Lima. He was committed to C.E.M.A.A. in every way, and was an evangelist. He had a vision and a hunger to use the hovercraft in

153

a new outreach. He was delightfully impatient, and persuasively intense.

Becky Pinto was married to Carlos. Young, slender and attractive, she brought with her a gentle stability that complemented Carlos' enthusiasm. She was the daughter of S.I.L. American missionaries, but had given up her U.S. citizenship to be committed for life to the Peru of her birthplace.

Sergio La Rosa was the last. Another young man, converted to Christianity from a life of drug addiction, Sergio was now in his last year at Lima Evangelical Seminary. He was an 'ordinary' man; handsome, stable, pleasant, keen; his presence immediately put everyone at ease. He also possessed the sort of physical power that could easily pull the hovercraft steering column off just trying to turn a corner.

Every one of these people was important; they were key people in the whole of Peru. There was a quality and potential about them that made Dick feel privileged to teach them.

They were at the Ops Centre before Dick, who puffed down the road after another of those incredible American breakfasts. At seven thirty a.m. on the dot, they looked over the hovercraft, and then went to a 'cool' room in the Translation Centre for lectures. The students asked so many questions that Dick only managed to complete the lecture on hovercraft principles, leaving the engineering aspects until another day. In any case, actually handling the craft would, of itself, answer questions on many of the difficult technical principles on which the hovercraft was based.

At eleven a.m. there was a dedication service for the hovercraft. Just about everyone was there, including children from the school. Mike Cole and Tito symbolically cut the Peruvian ribbon together.

Dick showed off the craft's capabilities to a few V.I.P.s. He started off with a 360° skidding turn, and a few emergency stops. He drove the craft over the water hyacinth to see how the River Rover would cope. This weed has been a curse all over the tropics. It floats on top of the water, and is blown about by the wind. It is a menace to the float-planes. Allen Wells had suggested importing manatees from Florida, which thrive on it, but that was a long-term solution. In the meantime, the hovercraft sailed over the weeds as if they were not there. The V.I.P.s were suitably impressed. Dick came back to the ramp, not knowing just how fast he needed to go to get up to the top. Mike stood in the middle of the ramp signalling him in. Dick frantically waved him away. Mike leaped aside as the hovercraft took the ramp at full throttle as if it were flat water. Rushing over the top, it flew another thirty metres up the runway on sheer momentum.

'Overdid that a bit,' Dick remarked wryly to his unnerved passengers as they clambered out on wobbly legs.

That afternoon, the instruction programme started in earnest. Dick used the same basic schedule for all the trainees. On the grass, they went round the craft, learning checks, and learning the position of all the controls. On the water, Dick took them through slow speed handling, first as a boat, then on the cushion. Then they went over hump speed, and learned the differences between driving under and over hump. How to stop; how to do a skidding turn; how to minimise skidding with the elevons but remain above hump. One by one, as the week progressed, the students became proficient and were sent 'solo'.

There was Tito, dripping with sweat as he found the hand-operated rudder control too heavy. Leo Lance, the flying instructor, could teach on the River Rover too, and probably in better Spanish than Dick's; he only needed half an hour before he went solo. Angel too learned quickly, but found the rudder control too stiff. He 'soloed' on Wednesday afternoon. Carlos went on Thursday morning, and had a fan blade break while he was solo: Dick had to borrow a *peci-peci* to help him out. Thursday afternoon was Stewart's turn. On Friday it was Sergio, who had never even driven a car; of all the Peruvians, Sergio had the best 'feel' for the skidding turn. Last of all, on Friday afternoon, there was Becky, with two cushions behind her so that she could reach full travel on the elevon pedals.

The craft was fully utilised. Once Dick wearily finished his teaching in the late afternoon Leo would take out some of his J.A.A.R.S. pilots for instruction. The lectures in the technical aspects of the craft were taken by Roy. James found himself talking to the high school on basic hovercraft principles.

155

Roy and James had plenty of other work to occupy them. After the dedication service on Tuesday, for example, they had gone into Pucallpa to try to sort out the problems with the canoe. They retrieved the repaired 40 hp outboards, and took them down to Maxi and Horacio. They discussed the provision of fuel for the journey. Mike had said that we would provide them with five barrels of fuel, but they were pressing for eight. Horacio wanted to buy the 55 hp outboard for 500,000 *soles*, but Mike would not sell it for less than 600,000. If we did not take it home, it would cost the Expedition £800, over a million *soles*. Even at 600,000 we would be making a substantial loss. That evening, Maxi and Horacio came to S.I.L. to talk it over. Mike gently put his foot down. No more. By this time, they had been given a bonus on the wages we had agreed, five drums of fuel and money for three more; Mike had repaired all the outboard motors, given them the spare, provided a new propeller, and given them a tent each. They could go with our thanks, but no more goodies.

A number of missionary societies had given over the total responsibility of their work in Peru to Peruvians, and C.E.M.A.A. was the result. But they had a problem with the hovercraft. They were such a young organisation that they had neither funds nor expertise to service and maintain the hovercraft for the years ahead. Julian, up-river, had built an engineering headquarters. It would be a few years before C.E.M.A.A. could do that down-river. They were in a quandary. The extent to which they could be dependent on S.I.L. and J.A.A.R.S., with all of their expatriate facilities, had to be hammered out now. Dick's role in finding a solution to the sensitive problem was a strong one.

Tuesday nights were prayer meeting nights on the Station. Everyone on the camp was committed to pray for a translator in the jungle, and they all collected in their groups to pray for those to whom God had drawn them. It was good for the four visitors to join in praying for the Machiguengas.

Before leaving, Dick was keen to try to sort out the problem of the stiff rudder. The rudder was pivoted at the leading edge. When the craft was stationary, it was easy to turn it. But when the fans were turning, and airflow was passing over the control surface, it made the rudder hard to turn, as the wind was resisting the deflection. Dick's idea was to rivet a curved piece of aluminium on to the leading edge of the rudder, ahead of the pivot point. This would create an aerodynamic force to help lighten the control, and save a lot of unnecessary hard work. Unfortunately, it was impossible in the time available, mainly for reasons of red tape rather than engineering. The modification had to be delayed until a time when the hovercraft would be laid up in the rainy season.

The social life in Yarinacocha was demanding. Everyone wanted the Britishers to eat with them. After an initial double booking, Betty Snell co-ordinated their lives. They had breakfast in five different homes, lunch in two, and supper in four! All their hosts were fascinating people. Al was in charge of the station electricity, water and vehicles; that was his missionary calling. Boyden was a carpenter, and did the house maintenance on the station. Kent and Michelle were there for a year: he looked after the hardware store, and she helped with translation (she was born in Mexico). He was a chemistry graduate, and would be returning to work for a doctorate (Ph.D.).

Tom Moore was the school headmaster. His wife Aureol was one of the few Britons on the station. They had lived extraordinary lives: God caught up with them in Ecuador, where the hippy trail had led them to a plentiful source of hard drugs. Now they were missionaries. Aureol gave her guests roast beef and Yorkshire pudding for supper – sheer nostalgia.

Roy co-ordinated a list of the modifications that they thought desirable and essential to the efficiency of the hovercraft. In our three months, we had been doing most of the tropical trials on the machine, and our report was crucially important to the design of further craft. Overheated people and hot engines, heavy rudders and a loose canopy; dealing with these would ease life considerably. Stewart took note of the suggestions. C.E.M.A.A. would, of course, need to approve them. And the engineering side of J.A.A.R.S. would be delighted to fit them, and to alter the craft to make it more efficient. John Bush had all sorts of other engineering suggestions to make as well. He thought it would be circumspect to inhibit it against termites, which will eat through wood (and particularly three-ply) in a

157

day. He also suggested that the underside be foam-sprayed to waterproof it. All these things had to be recorded, and left for another time. But the four prayed about the modifications, feeling that they could rely on God's memory more than on that of humans.

Mike left for Lima on Friday night. He had business with the Embassy and with the Bishop of Peru. For the others, too, the week was drawing to a close. On Saturday morning the team stood the hovercraft on oil drums to try to stop the ants eating the wood and the rats from eating the skirt.

The pace wound down. Dick presented certificates to the hovercraft drivers, announcing that they had qualified on the River Rover on the rivers of Peru. They relaxed, playing softball, and visited each other's hosts for a farewell supper. There were almost too many new friends to say goodbye to. In just a week they had come to know so many hospitable, selfless people. The place would remain in their, and our, memories for ever.

As they left, they were blessed with the most beautiful sunset of the whole expedition. Crimson covered the whole western sky, extending across the dome to the east. Palm trees and house tops were silhouetted black against this radiant and exquisite backdrop like a picture postcard of Bethlehem, etched indelibly on their minds as a permanent reminder of the extraordinary privilege they had just enjoyed.

The fact that they had to wait at Pucallpa airport for most of the night seemed unimportant. To the west there was a non-stop succession of lightning flashes, sometimes sudden and brilliant, sometimes covering the whole sky and illuminating the thunderstorms that hammered the Andes. The seven p.m. flight arrived at eleven forty-five p.m., and Aeroperu announced that they would not leave until the thunderstorms had cleared. They slept fitfully, lulled to sleep by some drunken Peruvians who sang love songs to a guitar's accompaniment. Aeroperu encouraged them by allowing them to sit in the F.28 at four a.m. and then took off at five a.m. – only ten hours late!

CHAPTER TWELVE

Mission Accomplished

THE LAST TIME any of us had seen Chris Bunney and Tim Hollis had been at San Francisco, as they climbed aboard a dilapidated four-ton truck, loaded with the remains of what had been our Base Camp. After the South American fashion, the so-called 'rear party' in fact left well before the 'main party' was even ready to depart. This state of affairs did not last, though, for the truck travelled only half a mile before the driver stopped at a café to take breakfast.

The task that Mike had set for the pair was to 'ride shotgun' on the truck, and see our equipment safely to Lima. We would meet up again in the capital, a few days before flying home. Their route would be San Francisco–Ayacucho–Pisco–Lima.

Since Chris had driven our Land Rover along the San Francisco–Ayacucho road himself, it held no particular surprises for them, even in the heavy truck. But after their night at the Hostal Santa Rosa in Ayacucho, the route took them across the High Andes. That was a different matter.

Initially, the road was good – not metalled, but smooth – as it wound its way up and around the hill overlooking Ayacucho. After forty-five minutes, they were still looking down at the town. But then the road deteriorated, as it started to cross the *puna*, the high plains of the Andes, gashed time and time again by valleys so deep that the valley floor could not be seen. Often, on apparently inaccessible ledges and shoulders, they could make out tiny isolated houses and patches of cultivation. The road got worse, and worse . . . and worse.

Just as they were starting to think 'this is ridiculous', and the road dropped precipitously into another valley, road markings and signs appeared warning 'Dangerous Road', 'Go Carefully', 'Hairpin Bend'.

'Oh, no,' groaned Tim. 'If they say *that*, they really must mean it.'

The road was a continuous series of bends, with the ground falling away near-vertically for thousands of feet below on one side, and precarious rock overhangs on the other.

If two vehicles met, one had to reverse, the driver's vision clouded by dust. The wheels were always close to the unfenced, crumbling road edge, but on one occasion a front wheel went over it, as the driver tried to pass another truck.

'He's going over the edge,' called Chris to Tim, rather less than casually. The driver slammed on air brake and hand brake, stopping with three wheels on firm ground. Chris opened his door to look down. 'Whew-w-w!' he exclaimed. The drivers of the two vehicles got together to decide how to retrieve the situation; the R.A.F. Squadron Leader and the Metropolitan Police Inspector decided to go for a quiet walk!

The heavy load on the truck, they decided, was a boon in situations like this, as the traction on the dirt roads was generally good enough to keep (or get) them out of trouble. Later, when they arrived on the Pan American highway between the vineyards of Ica and the coastal town of Pisco, they were less certain; the main leaf of the truck's front suspension had broken during the mountain crossing. The driver seemed unconcerned.

This was now the third day since the Apurímac. Worried about the driver's increasingly erratic driving after eighteen hours at the wheel, they had called a halt and spent an uncomfortable night sleeping on top of the truck in the mountains. Tim, cramped between an oil drum and some wooden panelling, had dreamt he was at a party in London telling someone about his night on a truck in the Andes; he woke to find he was still there. After a four a.m. start, they reached Pisco at daybreak, and Lima at midday. Much of their remaining daylight was spent in a frustrating search for the place where our equipment was to be stored. Having found that, and having spent the next day on the long list of 'Lima jobs' Mike had given them, their remaining time was their own.

Every member of the team had some plan of what to do with the week that would be free if everything went smoothly. For most, the magnetic attraction was the ruined city of Machu Picchu, and Tim and Chris were no exception. Their plans had gone through many a change; they had originally been members of a group of five from our team with an ambitious plan to trek from the Apurímac valley to Machu Picchu instead of travelling to Pucallpa. Just before our departure down-river, the group had broken up. Partly it was a result of the different expectations within the party; some saw it as a chance to see the sights, others – especially Allen Wells – as a test of endurance. But one reason seemed to be a growing lack of rapport between Cathy White and Allen. These two strong personalities seemed to clash more and more often; they decided that they might not work well together in a small group.

The latter stages of an expedition are not simply a test of physical strength or character. They are certainly that, but they also stretch our ability to get on with other people. Their habits and opinions start to get on our nerves, and the interactions of personality are a psychologist's paradise. We certainly did not develop any lifelong feuds among the team, but the patience of everyone was stretched taut. I, for one, found myself becoming more impatient as the weeks went on.

The team, then, needed and deserved the break. Chris and Tim flew to the ancient Inca capital of Cuzco and started to walk the four-day 'Inca Trail' to the Machu Picchu ruins. Allen made a similar walk, alone, and at a punishing pace, after we had moved out of Yarinacocha.

I, too, was keen to see more of the archaeological marvels of Peru, if possible; when Mike decided that Dick Bell would stay and carry on with the week's training at the S.I.L. base, I got my chance. At the last minute, I joined the two doctors.

'You seem eminently qualified to travel with us,' remarked Horace in mock condescension, 'on account of three attributes: your Spanish, your *South American Handbook* . . . and your credit card.' If we were to carry out the plan which combined both David's and my aspirations in just one week (Horace was content simply to follow our suggestions), then the blue, white and gold strip of plastic would be essential. It might be the only thing separating us from vagrancy.

Getting away from Lima was the acid test. We flew in from Pucallpa on Monday evening; if we did not get away to Cuzco on the early-morning flight on Tuesday, we would never fit everything in. The flight was scheduled at six-thirty, before the banks opened, and our jungle weeks hadn't left us enough cash for the tickets. At five forty-five a.m. we were in the Aeroperu queue at Lima airport.

'Seats? Yes, plenty,' said the girl. 'Credit card? No, sorry, you'll have to go to our town office at nine o'clock.' Dejected, we turned away, rejecting the advances of a friendly ticket tout who was very happy to sell us a ticket – for cash. With the two doctors, I walked the length of the terminal and back again, scanning from side to side for a travel agency that could perhaps sell a ticket. Nothing.

Belatedly, a thought crossed my mind: 'Have I prayed about this?' I had not; silently, I committed the problem to God. I looked up at the 'Departures' board; under the Aeroperu flight details was another flight to Cuzco. The 'other' Peruvian airline, Faucett, was scheduled to fly there at about the same time. I walked over to their desk.

'Credit card, sir? Certainly.'

'Do you know,' said David later, as we settled into the narrow BAC 1-11 seats, 'moments before you decided to go to the Faucett desk, I suddenly prayed for help.'

'So did I,' I said thoughtfully, 'so did I.'

The city of Cuzco, from which the Inca empire spread its tentacles through South America, lies at 11,000 feet above sea level. The wise visitor rests for a few hours after arrival to acclimatise, for *la soroche*, the nausea and pounding headache of altitude sickness, strikes especially at those who ascend quickly by plane. The three of us rested, and also tried a cup of *mate de coca*, coca leaf tea, which is said to alleviate some of the symptoms. I felt quite safe in this medical experiment with such highly qualified companions; the results were inconclusive.

Almost every street of the ancient city has Incaic walls or

archways alongside the sixteenth-century colonial buildings and the twentieth-century hovels, but the highlight of our week was Machu Picchu. To climb out of the steep-sided Urubamba canyon, our train from Cuzco had to ascend a switch-back track in a zig-zag until the 'saddle' was reached, at a height of 13,860 feet. From then on, the train progressed gently downhill and we were captivated by breathtaking views.

Later we stood among the ruins and marvelled.

'It's not until you get here that you understand how the place could have been undiscovered for four hundred years,' I said. The city stands on a saddle of the Huayna Picchu mountain and overlooks the roaring Urubamba river as it sweeps around in a loop two thousand feet below, almost encircling the Inca eyrie. From the valley, the city is invisible, and the Spaniards never found it; in 1911, American explorer Hiram Bingham stumbled across it almost entirely by accident. Today, the purpose of Machu Picchu is still shrouded in mystery, and the air of intrigue was emphasised for us by the grey mists hanging over the mountains.

The Inca civilisation challenges our ideas about the meaning of the word civilised. They did not use the wheel, yet they built suspension bridges and complex irrigation systems. They built immense earthquake-proof walls where the giant stone blocks, weighing up to thirty tons apiece, fit together so tightly that a knife-blade will not pass between them. The Incas were masters of road-building and architecture, of astronomy and social planning. Yet the civilisation was conquered as much by its own fratricidal divisions as by Pizarro's tiny army; today nothing remains but ruined cities and a folk memory.

Next day, we continued our lightning tour with what is said to be the 'most beautiful train journey in all the world' over the high plains for twelve hours to the bleak town of Puno, on Lake Titicaca, the world's highest navigable lake.

From our first-class seats (£5 for the full journey), we gazed out at mile upon mile of rolling *altiplano*. The cold, forbidding plain, beautiful in its severity, was interspersed by lively station halts. At each one, Quechua or Aymara women sold alpaca hats or sweaters and braided multicoloured belts. At one station, an enormous woman squatted on the platform, unwrapped a newspaper bundle, and proceeded to sell chunks of cooked llama meat from it.

Every new bargain made Horace wish he had not bought the last one, as his collection of gifts to carry home grew at each station. He did manage to resist the llama meat, though.

Puno was a disappointment, we all agreed, but its main attraction, a chance to visit the floating islands of the Uros Indians of Lake Titicaca, had been an ambition of David Langley for years. The ambition was realised, and we moved on, again by rail, to the beautiful white-stone city of Arequipa, an oasis of green in the midst of the forbidding desert on the western slopes of the Andes. There we visited a missionary couple from Nottingham, Barry and Anthea Harrison (Horace persisted in calling them 'Harry and Cynthia') who are supported by my home church.

Barry entertained us with stories of the Peruvian way of life. In terms of bureaucracy, retrospective laws were particularly novel. On one occasion, Barry had to pay a retrospective tax, *plus* the interest on the sum he should have paid the previous year (before the law was enacted), *plus* a fine for not paying it on time. Similarly, when he first arrived in the country one November and registered for employment, he was immediately fined for not having made the standard annual registration the previous March – eight months before he arrived.

We travelled the 1030 kilometres back to Lima by bus, exhilarated by all we'd seen.

The rest of the team were also converging on Lima from all points of the compass. Carlos Lopez, the Lima manager of British Caledonian (known to the British community as Carlos McLopez, for his habit of turning up at parties in full Scottish regalia, including B. Cal. kilt) had arranged for us to stay for our last three days at a very comfortable hotel at cheap rates. As each group arrived, stories were exchanged about their exploits.

Everyone seemed to have just missed everyone else in Cuzco, although few had crammed as much into the time as our little group. Some had had to work: Doug described how he had been setting up the Lima end of the Amazon Trust's radio link with the Apurímac, while Dick, Roy, James and Mike bubbled over with their experiences at Yarinacocha. Ricardo Ball had rushed off to visit his sister in some remote corner of the jungle.

One group, consisting of Cathy, Andy and Stuart Forbes, had supported R.E.M.E. Sergeant Jim Mudie in his attempt to gain the world altitude record for boardsailing, his favourite sport. They used a hired four-wheel-drive vehicle to get up to Lake Choclococha (15,100 feet) in the High Andes. Jim set up the windsurfer and surfed over the lake a few times, but soon started to feel the effects of the altitude and the exertion. The 'support team' quickly got him down to a lower altitude, but he had achieved his ambition, and the achievement will appear in the Guinness Book of Records 1984.

The last week had been a time for me to reflect on our work, and also on the individuals within the team. An expedition is one of those times when we have to accept each other 'warts and all', and it seemed to me that we had succeeded.

By the nature of the work we were doing, there were often two distinct groups in the team, the engineers and the medics, with other members oscillating between them from day to day. The division was clearly felt, especially among the engineering half, but their jokes about the 'A' team and 'B' team always stopped just short of being serious. The most disturbing times were when this vague division was from time to time seen to exist on the basis of religious belief, or of officer rank.

The Christian element had always been present, and the project's central inspiration had always been clear to every member. Not every member shared Mike's Christian belief. One thing was heartening, though. The most outspoken Christian on the team, Dick Bell, whose Hallelujahs had grated on many an ear, seemed by the end of our time to have won most of them over by his irrepressible enthusiasm and his genuine sincerity.

Every member had his or her contribution to make, and the team had hung together as a coherent unit. Mike Cole's decision to include female members had been vindicated by their resilient contribution and by their ability to be full members of the predominantly male team.

'Once you have humbly told God,' Mike challenged the team one night, 'that you have set no limits to what you are

165

prepared to do or where you are prepared to go, then, in the crisis, He will give you strength.'

I had found this to be true in the preceding months, and I, like many others, had learned from our experiences. Mike's concept of 'adventure with a purpose' was nothing new. It was a rediscovery of the ideas of explorers like Livingstone. Even further back in history, the apostle Paul was exposed to ship-wreck and countless other dangers to press his purpose forward. Mike Cole's lonely position of leadership required the same unyielding resolve. With him, we learned hard lessons. At times we had to step out in trust, swimming where it seemed foolish even to paddle, yet through the long summer we also needed the much more elusive quality of patience. It was a hard trial for many of the team, but also an experience gained.

There were other gains. In our attempt to break the per-manence of their poverty, we established an empathy with the Campa and Quechua Indians of the Apurímac which we shall treasure. In particular, the gentle, uncomplicated Campas perhaps made some of us change our ideas about civilisation.

'There's no such thing as tropical medicine,' said Bill Gould once, 'there's only the medicine of poverty.' We had made a small contribution to the valley people's fight against their hostile environment, where death and beauty vie constantly for attention. We had not completely solved their problems, and neither had we made no impact at all. This story cannot have the neatly rounded shape of a novel, for it is about true life. It is the story, simply told, of a few steps along a road, but a road where the centre line is marked by the thread of God's involvement.

We achieved each of our planned objectives to a depth which could not have been planned with human wisdom. The team, which included one who had served with the Falklands 'task force', had spent three months meeting the challenge of the violent moods of the river whose rapids, whirlpools and boulder banks cause havoc amongst the tribes-people. The success of the expedition had hinged on the performance of our Land-Rover-sized hovercraft.

The expedition's doctors and dentists had set up appropriate medical programmes staffed by Peruvian *sanitarios* at eleven riverside locations. The team engineers had installed radios into the clinics to link the service with base and the hovercraft. Tackling the root cause of much disease, members of the team had installed clean water supplies at three villages.

As an adventure we had taken our hovercraft through the giant *barrial* rapids in the narrow headwaters region of the Amazon. We had then completed a 1000-kilometre journey north through some of the wildest stretches of Amazonia. Peruvians had been trained to drive and maintain the hovercraft which will provide the on-going services, one in the headwaters and the other at Pucallpa in the heart of the dense jungle region. They will now be supported by two British Charities, the Amazon Trust and the Regions Beyond Missionary Union. These regions formerly beyond relief have now been brought within the scope of medical care by the British hovercraft, proved by this Joint Services Expedition, and backed by many loyal supporters who had prayerfully upheld the team throughout.

There are still loose ends. In the long term, the doctors feel, the medical work would benefit from a few years from a dedicated expatriate doctor to establish the work firmly. As yet, no such person has appeared.

In engineering, too, our few weeks of training were only a start, and here we have tried to ensure the continuation of the work. In July 1983, Gordon Davies went to Peru to spend up to two years, employed by the O.D.A., building up the engineering expertise of the Amazon Trust mechanics; Gordon had headed the Dodnor Marine work building River Rover, and his depth of experience and excellent Spanish make him ideal for the job. The future of Dodnor Marine is uncertain, as recession has dried up possible markets for the innovative River Rover.

In the Apurímac valley, the medical service up to Lechemayo will be met by the canoes, and the hovercraft will form a vital part in Julian's overall strategy of bringing a health service out into the distant, remote Ene, Perene and Tambo valleys. To add complication and uncertainty, the influence of the *Sendero Luminoso* terrorists has been increasing in San Francisco, and the health service may become a target.

167

And what of Mike Cole's irrepressible enthusiasm in the future? Well, there's the rest of Peru to open up, and a dream of navigating the mighty Yangtze river in mainland China. It is enough to remain open to leading and to retain a flexible mind.

One thing he finds difficult to get used to is the official recognition and cooperation he has been receiving. In the Queen's Birthday Honours List 1983, he was awarded an O.B.E., an honour he characteristically attributes to the efforts of the team. Yet our work had been receiving attention even before we left Peru.

The climax of the expedition had been a complete surprise to us. President Belaúnde had asked Mike to report our progress to him. But when we returned to Lima we found that the interview had been expanded into a formal luncheon for the British Ambassador, twelve team members and the B.B.C.'s Latin America correspondent, Harold Briley.

Harold Briley's ear for news is keen. In March 1982, he had repeatedly drawn attention to Argentinian invasion preparations. His distinctive voice, reporting from Buenos Aires, had become a familiar part of the Falklands campaign. Now he had rushed to Peru to report this 'task force for peace'! The resourceful journalist persuaded the Palace to add an extra seat to the lunch table.

Regrettably the team's invitation was for 'officers only', reinforcing a divide which had played little part in our work in the jungle, but Mike gave Roy Millington a 'promotion for the day' so that the engineers' leader would not be excluded.

On Wednesday, November 24th, many wearing borrowed jackets and ties, we arrived at the Presidential palace. Instead of the usual 10p, I had paid nearly £1 to have my jungle-stained, river-soaked Clarks boots raised to a suitably Presidential shine by a street shoeshine boy. As we climbed the ornate sweep of marble steps, between immaculate ceremonial guards in polished brass helmets, we looked exactly what we were – hastily respectabilised jungle explorers.

The President met us in an ante-room hung with twenty-foot gold velvet curtains, caught into the sides of the huge windows by golden tassels. The ceiling was embellished with intricate Italianate designs, while gold-embossed chairs stood

primly on a tightly-woven Turkish carpet. Liveried waiters
brought round cocktails and savoury canapés, which we took
to be our lunch. President Belaúnde's easy casual style and
excellent English made us feel relaxed in the stiff, formal
surroundings, as he chatted about his gratitude for our contribution to his country. Just as he had at Puerto Ocopa for
Channel 7 TV, he pushed aside any pretence that we were
anything other than servicemen.

Later, the President led us into a small dining room for the
real lunch, the best I have ever tasted. Over the *sole veronique*
and the *tournedos chasseur*, the President spoke in glowing terms
of the contribution the expedition had made. He coupled our
adventure with previous British efforts in Peru, connecting
us with such distinguished names as Markham and Toynbee.
Expressing warm greetings to our patron, Mr. Edward Heath,
he emphasised the success of our venture in promoting Anglo-
Peruvian relations, as well as its more direct health benefits.

Later, in an interview with Harold Briley, President
Belaúnde repeated for the B.B.C. the glowing remarks he had
made at lunch, concluding with an invitation to Mrs. Margaret
Thatcher to visit Lima. The B.B.C. end-of-year review for
1982 described 'the remarkable story of the hovercraft expedition to Peru' as 'the most positive British action for the
restoration of good relations during this difficult year in South
America.'

Born in an atmosphere of defence cuts, launched in the
wake of the Falklands conflict, this British military expedition
to South America could not – in theory – have had worse
timing. Yet in the end, for our unplanned and unsought task as
envoys to Peru, the timing had been perfect.

It had been a privilege to serve on a project which helped in a
small way to break the stranglehold of poverty and which did
much for the restoration of Anglo-Peruvian relations at a time
when that was sorely needed.

After lunch, President Belaúnde had pointed out a tiny river
on a map and carefully asked Mike to consider taking a hovercraft up it. Squadron Leader Mike Cole smiled as he contem-
plated the privilege of meeting another of God's challenges.

'Yes,' he said, 'I think it could be done.'

Team Members

Squadron Leader Michael Cole, R.A.F., 47, *leader.*
Leading Airman (Phot) Stuart Antrobus, (R.N.), 26, *photographer/ engineer.*
Louise Arrow, 26, *nurse.*
Chief Technician Dick Ball, (R.A.F.), 36, *engineer/interpreter.*
Captain Alan Batty, R.C.T., 39, *logistics preparation.*
Squadron Leader Dick Bell, (R.A.F. retired), 45, *instructor pilot.*
Squadron Leader Chris Bunney, R.A.F., 45, *chief administrator.*
Flight Lieutenant Ernie Clark, R.A.F., 33, *logistics preparation.*
Petty Officer Doug Cooledge, (R.N.), 42, *engineer/radio installation.*
Flight Lieutenant Peter Dixon, R.A.F., 32, *pilot/deputy leader.*
Michael Duke (British Airways), 31, *development pilot.*
Corporal Stuart Forbes, (R.A.F.), 27, *engineer.*
Doctor Bill Gould, 49, *medical doctor.*
Lieutenant Commander Brian Holdsworth, R.N., 54, *rear party leader.*
Inspector Tim Hollis (Metropolitan Police), 31, *administrator.*
Doctor David Langley, 43, *medical doctor.*
Sergeant Tony Maher, (R.M.), 28, *Gemini coxswain.*
Sub-Lieutenant James McClune, (R.N.), 25, *water supply installation/Pucallpa liaison.*
Chief Petty Officer Roy Millington, (R.N.), 37, *chief engineer.*
Sergeant Jim Mudie, (R.E.M.E.), 31, *engineer.*
Surgeon-Lieutenant Andy Prosser, R.N., 25, *dentist.*
Doctor Horace Pile, 58, *medical doctor.*
Graham Roberts, 25, *bridge engineer.*
John Riden (Welsh Water Authority), 41, *water surveyor.*
Senior Aircraftman Paul Turton, (R.A.F.), 21, *engineer/interpreter.*
Chief Technician Bruce Vincent, (R.A.F.), 45, *engineer.*

Corporal Paul Watson. (R.A.F.), 23, *engineer.*
Surgeon-Lieutenant Catherine White, R.N., 26, *dentist.*
Petty Officer Allen Wells, (R.N.), 32, *engineer.*
Doctor Jan Wright (Queen Mary College, London), 33, *engineer.*
Doctor David Wood, 48, *medical doctor.*

Sponsorship

Financial sponsorship

The following companies, organisations and individuals supported the expedition financially:

The Highway Trust; The Hedley Trust; Joint Services Expedition Trust; Overseas Development Administration; NSS Newsagents Ltd; Brixham Baptist Church; Nuffield Trust for the Forces of the Crown; Douglas Civil Engineers; Lloyds Bank International; China Fleet Club; Bridge End Garage, Montrose; Major R. L. J. Pott; Major M. Patterson; Second Officer F. Heal W.R.N.S.; Mrs. Holton; Mrs. Childs; Dr. & Mrs. Langley (Snr.); Mr. & Mrs. C. Eddershaw.

Service units of team members and team members' personal contributions.

Sponsorship of equipment/services

The following companies and organisations donated or loaned their equipment or services to the expedition:

Renault (U.K.) Ltd. (engines & spares); Lucas Marine Ltd. (batteries & hovercraft instruments); N.S.S. Newsagents (special edition of *Journey to the Fourth World*); British Caledonian Airways (concessionary travel); Shell Oils Ltd. (lubricants); O.M.C. Ltd. (Johnson outboard engines); Stella-Meta Filters Ltd. (filtration equipment); Alcan Ltd. (aluminium extrusions); Northern Rubber (hovercraft skirt material); Land Rover Ltd. (cost price spares); Aeroelectronics (A.E.L.) Ltd. (loan of U.H.F. radios); R.B.N., Basingstoke (portable welding set); Rotary Club of Hull (Cansdale water pump); Honda (U.K.) Ltd. (portable generators); Chubb

Ltd. (fire safety equipment); Defence Public Relations (John Evans) (publicity services); London Fan Company (hovercraft fan blades); R.H.P. Ltd. (bearings); Wiggins Teape Ltd. (first day covers); Freightliner (free use of container); Milne & Co. (free return shipping of container); Fabrica La Union, Lima (storage of container); Hogg Robinson Ltd. (shipping arrangements); SpanSet Ltd. (lifting straps); C. T. Bowring Group (concessionary insurance); Goodyear Ltd. (drive belts for Mk. 2 craft); UniRoyal Ltd. (drive belts for Mk. 3 craft); Bridgedale Ltd. (cost price sweaters); Williams & Glyn's Bank, Farnborough (banking services); R.F.D. Ltd. (lifejackets); Miltech Ranger (electrical equipment); Ladyline Ltd. (oscillating fan); Frigidaire (battery refrigerators); Coopers Ltd. (gaskets); Panasonic Business Equipment Ltd. (micro-cassette recorders); Better Air Products Ltd. (cabin dehumidifier); Clarks Ltd. (jungle boots); Dolbys Ltd. (accounts book); Pilkington Ltd. (sunglasses); London Dinghy Centre (wetsuit); Cotswold Windsurfing (sailboard).

The following companies donated drugs or equipment to the medical work:

Armour Pharmaceutical Co. Ltd.; Ayerst Laboratories Ltd.; Bayer (U.K.) Ltd.; Brocades (G.B.); Bencard (Beecham Laboratories Research); Boehringer Ingelheim Ltd.; Boots Co. Ltd.; Bristol-Myers Co. Ltd.; Ciba-Geigy Pharmaceuticals Division; Duncan Flockhart & Co. Ltd.; Duphar Laboratories Ltd.; Eli Lilly Co. Ltd.; Glaxo Laboratories; I.C.I.; Janssen Pharmaceuticals Ltd.; Dista Ltd.; Kabivitrum Ltd.; Keymer Pharmaceuticals Ltd.; Leo Laboratories Ltd.; May & Baker Ltd.; Merrell Pharmaceuticals Ltd.; E. Merck Ltd.; Thomas Morson Ltd.; Organon Laboratories Ltd.; Pfizer Ltd.; Parke Davis & Co.; Reckitt Colman Ltd.; Stuart Pharmaceuticals Ltd.; Searle Laboratories; E. R. Squibb & Sons Ltd.; Syntex Pharmaceuticals Ltd.; Vickers Medical Ltd.; Zyma (U.K.) Ltd.

As Mike Cole says, our sponsors and supporters are all part of 'the wider team', without whom the whole venture would have been impossible. We thank them all most warmly.

APPENDIX THREE

Some Technical Considerations

by Jan Wright and Mike Duke

This appendix provides a brief introduction to hovercraft in general and the River Rover in particular; references 1–4 cover the subject in more detail. In addition, some comments on the overall performance of the craft in Peru will be made.

1. General comments

Hovercraft in use around the world vary in size from the single-seat sport craft to large seagoing craft such as the S.R.N. 4 weighing around 200 tons. The River Rover (see Fig. 1) is a relatively small six-seat craft with an empty weight of approximately 800 kg (1800 lb) and payload of 450 kg (1000 lb).

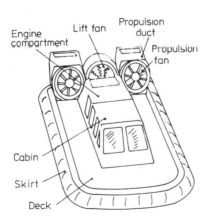

Fig. 1 Overall schematic view of the River Rover Mark 3 Hovercraft.

175

Hovercraft are a particular class of Air Cushion Vehicle in which the weight of the craft is supported on a pressurised cushion of air above the surface it is travelling over. Because the cushion pressure (1000 N/m² or 20 lbf/ft² for River Rover) is low, of the order of one-hundredth of the contact pressure of a car tyre on the road, the hovercraft is able to travel over water as well as land. Moreover, by containing the air cushion within a flexible 'skirt' and ensuring an adequate hover-height (i.e. clearance between the hard hull structure and the surface), the hovercraft can pass over protruding obstacles such as rocks and logs (up to 0.3 m or 1 ft high in the case of River Rover).

2. The hump problem

One of the problems associated with travelling over water is the phenomenon of 'hump'. The pressurised air in the cushion causes a weight of water equal to the weight of the craft to be displaced, and thus produces a trough or depression in the water beneath the craft. As the craft moves forward, the depression moves with it and a bow wave or 'hump' is formed just ahead of the craft, the size of the wave increasing with speed. However, a particular speed is reached where the wave can no longer 'keep up with' the craft; another way of thinking of it is that the craft effectively climbs over its own bow wave. This process of 'getting over hump' occurs at a relative speed between the craft and the water of around 10 knots (5 m/s, 11 m.p.h.) for River Rover. Because the retarding force (or drag) due to the wave reaches a maximum at the 'hump speed', considerable propulsive power is required at this stage.

Beyond the hump speed, the craft is able to 'skim' over the water at a lower and thus more economical power level. The overall maximum speed of the craft occurs when the maximum thrust balances the total retarding force due to a range of different drag factors.

3. The lift and propulsion system

Clearly a hovercraft requires power both to provide the pressurised air cushion and to develop forward thrust. The lift and thrust are usually provided by ducted fans or propellers. On many craft there are separate engines for the lift and propulsion systems. However, for simplicity, the River Rover utilises a single Renault 20TX (2165 cc) petrol engine developing 109 b.h.p. at 5000 r.p.m.; it drives one central lift fan at the rear of the engine compartment and two thrust fans (one on each side of the craft at the rear) via rubber toothed belts (see Fig. 1). The fans used are the simple nylon-bladed Breeza axial-flow type where the direction of air flow is parallel to the axis of rotation of the fan.

The lift fan uses 12 blades set at a moderate angle to the plane of the fan (called blade pitch) and has to maintain the cushion pressure as well as providing sufficient airflow to replace leakage between the lower edge of the skirt and the surface; this leakage can be quite significant in the rough water encountered in rapids. The propulsion fans use six blades set at a higher pitch and aim to move as large a volume of air as fast as possible to produce the thrust required. The proportions of the engine power assigned to lift and propulsion in this integrated system can be controlled at the design stage by choice of fan size and speed (i.e. gearing), blade pitch and number of blades. Since to some extent the proportions required depend on the operating conditions, on-site adjustment of the blade pitches provides 'fine tuning'. For example, the rapids in Peru necessitated a somewhat higher proportion of the total power being assigned to lift than for smooth water operation (namely 45% as opposed to 40%).

4. The skirt

The design of the skirt system is a complex matter; the Hovercraft Development Ltd. 'loop and segment' skirt as used on River Rover is no exception. In essence, the pressurised air from the lift fan is directed around the circumference of the craft just beneath deck level in a flexible distribution duct (or 'bag') formed by the loop and diaphragm as shown in Fig. 2. The air is allowed to feed downwards into the cushion via various holes in the diaphragm; the cushion is mainly fed near to the bow in order to prevent the skirt collapsing on wave impact and the subsequent 'ploughing in' of the craft. The slope on the diaphragm and the front of the hull also help to prevent 'plough-in'. The cushion is contained within a curtain of flexible interconnected segments or 'fingers'. These are designed to minimise drag and to follow the contour of any obstacle as closely as possible, so reducing the air loss from the cushion.

5. Control

Clearly it is important to be able to control both the forward speed and direction of motion of hovercraft for operation below and above hump speed. However, due to the minimal contact of the craft with

177

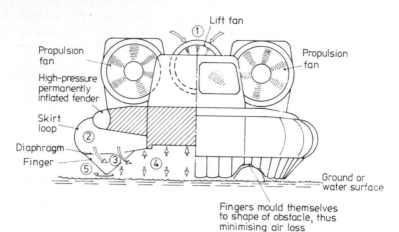

Fig. 2 Craft hovering.
1) Air drawn in and pressurised by lift fan at rear of craft.
2) Pressurised air carried forward through duct formed by flexible skirt loop and diaphragm.
3) Air fed through holes in forward part of diaphragm.
4) Relatively low pressure acting over large area lifts craft.
5) Fingers provide a flexible seal, minimising loss of lift air to atmosphere.

the surface, the control problem is severe and is arguably the major disadvantage of hovercraft today. Indeed, as yet there is no unified control concept for hovercraft, whereas there has been one for motor vehicles, aircraft and boats for some considerable time. The range of control techniques used is so wide and is so dependent on craft size that it is possible here only to make a few general comments.

Forward speed is reduced by controlling the thrust, normally whilst maintaining lift pressure; in an emergency the craft can be 'ditched' by cutting off the lift air flow. If there are separate lift and propulsion engines, then independent control of thrust is straightforward. Also, on large craft, reversible blade-pitch propellers are sometimes used to provide zero or reverse thrust. Small craft with a single engine either have to block off the thrust duct or to suffer a reduction in lift in order to reduce the thrust.

Direction of motion can be changed by use of vertical control surfaces (called rudders) in the slipstream of the propellers. However, the forces produced tend to roll the craft out of the turn, thus causing sideways slipping, and so rudders are rather ineffective. It is preferable to turn a hovercraft by causing it to roll or bank into the turn rather like an aircraft; this can be achieved either by swivelling the propellers about a vertical axis or by lifting or shifting the skirt on one side of the craft to alter the position of the cushion centre of pressure. These are both somewhat complex solutions to the problem.

The River Rover control concept is a unique and simple approach to the control problem, originated by Tim Longley; it is arguable that certain features of it could successfully be applied to much larger craft. The propulsion fans are each set in a short circular duct which helps to augment the thrust; the flow then enters a rectangular box-like duct with a gap in the roof (see Fig. 3). A large horizontal control surface called an elevon (because it combines the functions of an elevator and aileron as on a tail-less aircraft like Concorde) is placed centrally in each rectangular duct. When an elevon is rotated nose down about a pivot near to its centre, the air from the propulsion fan is deflected upwards through the roof gap; the craft thus experiences a downward force and a reduction in thrust on the same side, causing it to bank and turn effectively. A rudder is also placed at the rear of each duct, being required to assist control in cross-winds.

A bonus of the concept is that the elevons can be used to nullify

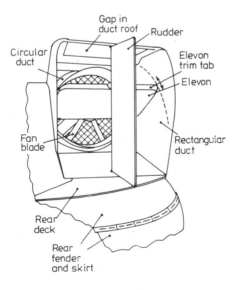

Fig. 3   View of the starboard propulsion duct from the rear showing the elevon and rudder arrangement.

179

the thrust without losing lift by rotating them so that they block off both ducts. Also, a low-speed manoeuvring capability is provided by operating the elevons independently.

It is this control system that enables River Rover to be handled with some degree of confidence, thus making negotiation of narrow winding rivers and rapids a possibility.

(It should perhaps be pointed out that the Mk. 3 version of River Rover taken to Peru differs from the Mk. 2 version used in Nepal in having a larger engine and fans, a different transmission arrangement, which meant that the engine was mounted lower in the hull, and also a rearrangement of the control layout in that the elevons and rudders are now controlled by foot pedals and a hand-operated 'yoke' respectively.)

6. Comments on operational aspects in Peru

During the time that the team spent in Peru, the two new craft logged about 150 operating hours, on short and long journeys, with a most encouraging reliability. However, there were a few teething problems, most significantly the overheating of the engine in the rather high ambient temperatures of 30–35°C. Because the engine is mounted fairly low down in the hull and is largely enclosed to protect it against spray, there was little cooling air flow over the exhaust and engine block, and so the radiator mounted downstream of the lift fan was unable to cope. The solution was to introduce scoops on both sides of the engine compartment above deck level at appropriate places and also to bleed pressurised air from the 'bag' into the engine area. However, even after this modification the bulkhead between the engine and the cabin remained very hot due to the proximity of the exhaust (even though there was some shielding) and the life of the nearby bilge pump was shortened; clearly some re-routing of the exhaust would be worth considering. One other problem occurred when some of the propulsion fan blades fractured due to the circular duct fixings working loose, a fairly simple matter to put right. There was no additional damage.

The skirt and hull sustained some damage fairly early on in operations as training pilots gained familiarity with the craft, particularly when bringing it on to land where large boulders abounded! However, repairs were fairly straightforward to carry out; the rubber material of the skirt can be repaired by stitching or patching whilst the hull construction of extruded aluminium alloy sections and marine plywood panels allows replacement of damaged components. Some small modification in the attachment position of the diaphragm of the skirt to the bottom of the hull is suggested, to avoid material becoming trapped under the hull and tearing when putting down on very rough ground; in such cases the four landing pads do not prevent ground contact elsewhere on the hull.

7. Comments on performance in Peru

The rapids, current, boulder banks and winds encountered on the Apurímac river provided a severe test of the performance and controllability of the River Rover with which it coped very well. Severe rapids with waves up to 1 m (3 ft) in height (peak to trough), and sometimes with much larger isolated standing waves, were negotiated safely with a good payload; the control system usually allowed the pilot to choose the best route through a rapid with some confidence. However, since there are very significant seasonal changes in the river (it rises about 10 m or 30 ft during the rains), making it even more dangerous, the operation of the hovercraft is likely to be limited at certain times and places on the river.

It is interesting to note that the presence of the river current (average of, say, 5 knots) meant that it was much easier to get over hump when travelling up-river against the current than down-river, since hump speed is related to the craft speed relative to the water and not to the river bank. Once over hump, the current has little effect. The wind experienced in the river valley of up to 20 knots (Force 5) was surprisingly high and introduced a significant effect on performance, depending obviously on whether it was a head- or tail-wind.

The craft taken to Peru were the first of the Mk. 3 version to be fitted with a lift fan modification in which the position of the fan was raised by about 0.25 m (9 in). This modification was aimed at improving the flow into the lower part of the fan and reducing the likelihood of fan 'stall'; previously the bottom of the fan was rather low in the engine compartment and the concern was that it was somewhat 'starved' of air. The evaluation of this modification indicated a noticeable improvement in the inlet flow field (using flow visualisation) and in the ability of the craft to get over hump more easily; it is clear and not really surprising that the lift fan was working more effectively.

Some simple but limited measures of craft speed, average journey speed and fuel consumption were made in Peru but the figures are approximate and are presented here to give some feel for the craft's performance. A range of figures is given because there are numerous factors which influence the performance, namely wind, payload, river condition (e.g. number and severity of rapids), direction of travel (up- or down-river), engine cruise r.p.m. setting and pilot experience.

Fuel consumption seemed to vary between about 4 galls/hr in cruise and 7 galls/hr when operating at maximum r.p.m. (as when climbing a rapid). However, average fuel consumption over a journey was more like 4–5 galls/hr.

Depending on payload, the craft was able to cruise at as low as 4000 r.p.m. (95 b.h.p.). Cruise speeds varied from about 16–27 knots and average journey speeds were of the order of 14–19 knots.

These journey speeds are roughly twice those achieved by the large canoes (18 m length) used on the river at certain times of the year. The canoes, powered by two 40 hp outboard motors, were clearly able to carry a substantially higher payload than the hovercraft for equivalent power, but have a number of disadvantages in addition to their speed; they have to take extreme care in shallow water (sometimes having to be pushed by hand) or near obstacles, and they are more dangerous, requiring very skilful and experienced boatmen with a detailed knowledge of the river.

It should be noted that the maximum payload of about 450 kg for the hovercraft includes passengers, baggage and fuel, so for longer journeys where extra fuel tanks are carried (giving an endurance of about 7 hrs) then the number of passengers is reduced. For various other reasons too, the craft seems most suitable for operating in Amazonia at a maximum radius of around 150 km from its base, and not for long distances.

Finally, whilst the basic concept of the craft is excellent and well-proven, there is still room for further improvement. For example, there are various possibilities for developing the control concept (such as introducing a reverse thrust capability). The thrust to weight ratio could be improved by fitting a set of flow-straightening blades behind each propulsion fan to increase the thrust, and by reducing the weight, particularly at the rear of the craft, by modification of the transmission unit. In addition, there are various detail design changes that would aid accessibility and maintainability in remote areas where facilities, spares and expertise can be limited.

References

1. *Journey to the Fourth World* by M. E. Cole, Lion 1981 (particularly the Appendices).

2. *Hovercraft and Hydrofoils* by R. McLeavy, Blandford 1976.
3. *Hovercraft Design and Construction* by G. H. Elsley and A. J. Devereux, David & Charles, Newton Abbot 1968.
4. 'Two Approaches to Controlling Hovercraft' by M. Cox and T. J. Longley, *Engineering*, July 1979.

APPENDIX FOUR

Medical Report

by the Medical Team
(Abridged from papers published in the *British Medical Journal*.)

The two areas with which the medical team were concerned were, firstly, the medical needs of expedition members before, during and after the expedition, and, secondly, the planning and delivery of the primary medical programme along the river by hovercraft. This appendix will deal with the two areas separately, although in practice they overlapped.

Team medicine

PREPARATION

In the months prior to departure, team members were advised to undertake physical fitness training. This period of preparation was additionally lengthened by the unexpected delay during the Falklands war. Nine months before the eventual departure, each member was acquainted with the various medical requirements, including inoculations; each person was then asked to produce evidence of a full recent physical examination, chest X-ray and dental examination, and to list any allergies and current medication. Thus an up-to-date record for everyone was available during and after the expedition.

At early team meetings the opportunity was taken to prepare the team medically. Vaccinations were given and on one occasion blood was drawn from each member for later comparison.

Inoculations advised were as follows: typhoid, cholera and tetanus; rabies (two injections of inactivated rabies vaccine at a month's interval as protection against bites from infected vampire bats, prevalent in the particular area); oral polio vaccine; yellow fever (ensures protection for 10 years); protection against hepatitis (3.4 ml dose of gamma globulin a week before departure), although we recognised that the benefit was relatively short-lived; malaria prophylaxis (Maloprim, taken once weekly – we chose the rest day, Sunday – from 2 weeks before departure until 4 weeks after return); lastly, members with a negative Heaf test were asked to have B.C.G. vaccination.

PERSONAL MEDICAL KIT

Each team member was issued with a personal medical kit containing: tropical health leaflet; antiseptic cream; assorted Elastoplast; salt tablets; water purification tablets; insect repellent; ant powder; paracetamol tablets; Senokot; Piriton; Lomotil; tetracycline; Maloprim; Flagyl; Chloroquin; morphine ampoule.

BASE CAMP

The main hazards at Base Camp soon became evident: bites and stings from the local fauna (snakes, spiders, insects, bats and scorpions) were of course a constant danger, but the priority was to get a clean, safe and reliable water supply for the team. The part of the river that served the town also received most of its waste material. Bacteriological analysis of the water indicated an extraordinarily high coliform count, plus protozoa and evidence of other contamination.

The expedition was fortunate in having the loan of an SB 4L portable water filtration plant supplied by Stella-Meta Filters Ltd. of Whitchurch, Hants. The system, weighing 83 kg, consisted of a petrol-driven pump drawing water through a stama filter and then through a flowmeter which added a measured proportion of chlorine solution; the system was exceptionally reliable and effective, and we believed that it played a significant part in preventing a major outbreak of gastro-enteritis.

However, on the 2–3 day trips to village clinics we were unable to take Base Camp water with us so it was necessary to fill a large container of water and treat it with sterilising tablets to give a residual chlorine, assessed by means of the simple water testing kit described in the Army Manual of Health.

CAMP ACCOMMODATION

Accommodation was in 3- or 4-man army tents, with a camp bed each. An essential was a mosquito net, not only to exclude mosquitos and possible malaria, but also to deter possibly rabid vampire bats. Members found that insect repellent cream was of questionable value in deterring mosquitos and other insects. Every person was encouraged to carry a good torch at night, even walking between tents, to avoid stepping on snakes etc.

LATRINES

Deep trench latrines were dug below base camp and 3 sufficed for the 3-month period. In addition, a separate urinal pit was dug. It was relatively easy to wash after leaving the latrines, for the washing area was close. Water for washing was taken from the river, allowed to settle, and then chlorinated to ensure relative cleanliness. Members were told it was not for drinking or teeth cleaning.

COOKING

Cooking and catering were overseen by 3 expedition members, but daily rotas enabled many members to assist with cooking and food preparation. Strict guidelines were laid down about scrubbing hands, and in the mess tent it was always possible to wash and disinfect using 2 separate bowls. Inevitably on trips down river, standards in food hygiene became less strict, but emphasis was always on using only safe water.

THE TEAM'S HEALTH

Two major illnesses developed amongst the 28 members. Within a week of arrival at base camp Corporal Watson became ill with the condition described at the beginning of Chapter 1. The second occurred towards the end of the time in San Francisco, when Tony Maher was struck with typhoid fever (see Chapter 7).

There were no cases of serious trauma or psychological disturbance amongst the team, and despite the high altitudes experienced in crossing the Andes, no true altitude sickness. However, breathlessness was noted on exertion at high altitudes, as well as cyanosis of finger nails and mild headache, but there were no instances of pulmonary oedema or severe headaches.

186

APPENDIX FOUR

POST EXPEDITION

At the conclusion of the expedition, each member was given a questionnaire to fill in concerning their health during the period in Peru. In accordance with Service Regulations, chest X-rays were carried out at 6 and 12 months post-expedition.

Delivery of primary medical care by hovercraft along the River Apurímac

In the medical work along the river, a pattern of working with the *sanitarios* in each village clinic was soon established (see Chapter 7). The *sanitarios*, young men and women who had received a nine-month government-run course in basic health care, varied in ability, but without doubt all had gained considerably in their medical knowledge and skills when we left, and this was, we believe, our greatest contribution to the expedition. The basic concept of training young people as health workers and auxiliaries has much to commend it, provided they are adequately supervised, encouraged and given means of communication with someone senior. Thus each clinic visit had a dual purpose; not only were people treated, but new knowledge and skills were constantly being passed on, and as relationships developed, the *sanitarios* began to select cases for us to see and discuss with them.

In the months of planning and discussion prior to departure, three books were particularly helpful: *Where there is no doctor* by Werner, *Medical care in developing countries* by Maurice King and *Paediatric priorities in the developing world* by D. Morley. It was decided to concentrate maximum effort on children under 5 and their mothers, realising that these were the groups at greatest risk. We were conscious that the service we had to establish should not be second-rate Western medicine but appropriate Third World medicine. We designed 3 different forms to help standardise our work in gathering statistics and in building up a picture of the disease pattern. The first form was used on our first visit to a village and provided information about village facilities, e.g. population, school, water supply etc. The second form was used to document information gathered on children aged 0–5 years, including a child's position in a family and the deaths of any other children in the family. The third form was a disease pattern chart, enabling us to record each patient's diagnosis and obtain a general picture of the commonest diseases.

At each clinic the under-5s and their mothers were given priority. In the Campa villages we could only begin to see patients when the

187

chief had given the word. Each child was weighed and its height measured and arm circumference checked. Using a strip of old X-ray film from which the emulsion had been removed, marks were made at 0 cm, 12.5 cm and 13.5 cm. Up to 12.5 cm the film was coloured red, between 12.5 and 13.5 it was coloured yellow, and past 13.5 it was coloured green. A child's upper arm circumference is almost the same between the ages of 1 and 5 years, so when the middle of the upper arm is measured in this age group, one can find the malnourished children. Similarly, using the Nabarro Weight for Height chart, an index of malnourishment is provided and children at risk can be spotted. Each mother was given a simple 'Road to Health' card kept in a polythene envelope, which was closely guarded by the mothers and brought to the clinic at each visit.

Many children had worms – ascaris, threadworm or hookworm – and it become almost routine to offer treatment for parasites even if the mother did not mention the problem.

FINDINGS

In the under 5 age group we recorded:

Parasitic infection in	32%
Respiratory infections in	30%
Gastro-enteritis in	20%
Skin infections in	15%
Severe malnutrition in	8%

One helpful item in teaching mothers about the need for fluid replacement in gastro-enteritis was a simple plastic spoon with a large measure at one end for sugar and a small measure at the other end for salt. Mothers were instructed to make up a simple dehydration drink using boiled water mixed with a measure of both salt and sugar. When the supply of spoons ran out, mothers were recommended to mix the boiled water with enough sugar to fill the cupped palm of the hand, and as much salt as could be held in the dip of the thumb nail.

Our policy of majoring on the under-5s was justified retrospectively when analysis of our statistics indicated a very high mortality rate in this group. Our observations suggest that the 3 commonest causes of death in the crucial early days and weeks of life were (1) neo-natal tetanus and septicaemia because of dirty and inadequate delivery techniques, (2) malnutrition as mother's milk dried up and (3) respiratory infections progressing to fatal pneumonia.

Nutritional state of children under five
We found evidence of malnutrition in 40% and severe malnutrition in 8%. Children between 1 and 3 years are particularly at risk when another child is born into the family, and they are weaned off the breast. There was a 42% mortality rate in children under 5 (compared with 1% in U.K.). This was a random sample of 100 families from the 11 clinics we visited.

After very young infants, the next group we studied was the 5 to 15 age group. Here, parasitic infections were even higher, and pulmonary tuberculosis was not uncommon. Skin infections, gastro-enteritis and dysentery were relatively common. In this age group (both sexes) the disease pattern was as follows:

Intestinal parasites	48.5%
Respiratory infections (including T.B.)	13.5%
Gastro-enteritis	7.5%

The disease pattern in adults showed little variation between the sexes. One obvious difference was the incidence of anaemia in women due to a combination of factors such as frequent pregnancies, little or no antenatal care and gynaecological abnormalities, as well as hookworm anaemia.

Both males and females had a high incidence of peptic ulcer symptoms, higher in males because of drinking habits and possibly the chewing of coca. As in the West, low back pain was frequent in both sexes. We saw very few cases of yellow fever and hepatitis, and heard of, but never saw, cases of rabies or people who had snake bites.

Top 10 diseases in males

Dyspepsia	19%
Low back pain	16%
Chest infections	13%
Trauma	10%
Skin infections	8%
Intestinal parasites	5%
'Vague ill health' syndrome	5%
T.B. chest	4%
Upper respiratory tract infection	4%
Urinary tract infection	4%

Top 10 diseases in females

Low back pain	15%
Dyspepsia	14.5%
Chest infection	9%
Anaemia (including hookworm)	9%
Urinary tract infection	8%
Skin infections	8%
'Vague ill health' syndrome	5.5%
Dysentery	4.5%
Eye infections	4%
T.B. chest	3%

THE FUTURE

Using hovercraft and radios to link clinics to a base has the potential for providing a first-class primary medical service. However, to be realistic, the future of the service depends on the motivation of the Peruvians themselves, who will have the responsibility when the Europeans have left. It depends on the reliability and efficiency of the Peruvian doctors and nurses and *sanitarios* who must provide a caring service. It depends on the Peruvian pilots and engineers who must drive and maintain the craft. It depends on those who carry out the day-to-day administration.

We have proved that it can be done and demonstrated how, with the right stimulus and motivation, needs can be met.

RECOMMENDATIONS

1. That the 'Hover Doctor' service, delivering primary health care along the Apurímac river, continue.
2. That the children under 5 and their mothers should remain the number-one priority.
3. That a full vaccination programme, according to Peruvian Government regulations, be encouraged in the under-5s.
4. That each village should be offered help, so long as it is matched by help from the community itself, in installing a safe and clean water supply.
5. That the *sanitarios* continue to learn from an ongoing teaching programme. The seminar that we arranged could be repeated 2 or 3 times a year. It makes sense to involve the schoolteachers in health care in villages where no *sanitario* as yet exists.

6. That efforts be made to strengthen the San Francisco base and develop the hospital there, as a centre for patients the *sanitarios* are unable to help.

7: That only a basic number of medicines and supplies be used and stocked in each clinic, to simplify treatment and care. The concept of the 'Top 20' drugs is a pattern to follow, although there will be problems in implementing this.

THE RIVER MEDICAL SERVICE — 'TOP TWENTY' DRUGS

1. Analgesic   Aspirin or Panadol tab
2. Penicillin   Injections/tab/syrup
3. Metronidazole tab
4. Oxytetracycline tab
5. Chloromycetin tab
6. Pripsen syrup
7. Vermox tab
8. Cough mixture
9. Multivitamin tab
10. Iron tab
11. Chloroquin tab
12. Antacid tab or liquid
13. Piriton tab
14. Benzyl Benzoate liquid
15. Steroid skin cream
16. Antiseptic skin cream
17. Anti-fungal cream
18. Eye ointment
19. Vaginal cream and pessaries
20. T.B. medicine   INH/TZ combination

                              Dressings
                              Tape
                              Suture Kit
                              Savlodil
                              Gloves
                              KY jelly
                              Syringes/needles/sterets

Chronology of Events

Dec. 78–Mar. 79	Joint Services Hovercraft Expedition to Nepal
1 Jul. 79	First broadcast of B.B.C. film *Journey to the Fourth World*
Jun. 81	Cole/Dixon reconnaissance to Apurímac Valley
Jan. 82	Team selection; stand at London Boat Show
1 Apr. 82	Cole visit to Lima
1 May–28 Jul. 82	Intended dates of Expedition to Peru (delayed by Falklands war)
9 Sep. 82	Team departs Gatwick for Lima
13 Sep. 82	Team travels Lima–Ayacucho–San Francisco
14 Sep.–5 Nov. 82	Establishment of clinic service; training of pilots/engineers
4 Oct. 82	Dr. Bill Gould makes first medical trip in hovercraft to Sivia
17 Oct. 82	Official Inauguration of Medical Service
29/30 Oct. 82	06 travels to Puerto Ocopa at President's request and 05 makes up-river exploration
2 Nov. 82	Hovering Medical Service operated by Peruvians. Dr. David Langley as passenger
6/7 Nov. 82	Medical Symposium for teachers and health workers
8/12 Nov. 82	Journey to Pucallpa. Overnight struggle through *caño*
13 Nov. 82	Arrive Wycliffe Translators camp at Yarinacocha
18 Nov. 82	Jim Mudie at Lake Choclococha: World Altitude Windsurfing Record
24 Nov. 82	Lunch at Presidential Palace
26 Nov. 82	Arrival Gatwick
5 May 83	Report meeting, Royal Aeronautical Society, London
Queen's Birthday Honours List 1983	Mike Cole awarded O.B.E.